STUDIES IN ENGLISH LITERATURE

Volume XVI

FORTUNA AND NATURA

A Reading of
Three Chaucer Narratives

by

BARBARA BARTHOLOMEW
Houston, Texas

1966
MOUTON & CO.
LONDON · THE HAGUE · PARIS

Printed in The Netherlands

ACKNOWLEDGEMENTS

I should like to express gratitude to the Southern Teaching Career Fellowships Fund, to Professor R. M. Lumiansky, and especially to my husband.

BARBARA BARTHOLOMEW

TABLE OF CONTENTS

I. INTRODUCTION

In almost all of his poems, Chaucer makes some mention of the Goddess Natura or the Goddess Fortuna or both. Scholars accordingly have noted the complexity which these mighty allegorical figures frequently assume in Chaucer's works. Though much scholarly work has been done on the concepts of Fortuna and Natura, the functional roles of the goddesses and their dynamic relationship to each other in Chaucer's narratives have not been fully investigated. A glance at the *Concordance* [1] indicates that Chaucer makes more use of Fortuna-than Natura-as-deity; however, singly or as a pair, the goddesses appear with almost every possible function in Chaucer's poetry. On most occasions they are the stereotyped figures invoked in conventional formulae, whether for serious or satiric purpose: for example, the "Merchant's Tale" (IV. 1312-1314, 2057-2064) and the "Melibeus" (VII. 1446-1457 [2]). This study will not treat the narratives in which references to Natura and Fortuna seem merely conventional. Frequently in the narratives they appear within an orthodox Christian framework, serving emphatically as the agents of the Christian God (the "Parson's Tale" and the "Man of Law's Tale"). Occasionally, though their subservience to God is mentioned, they appear as destinal figures almost absolute in their own authority (the "Monk's Tale" and the *Parliament of Fowls*).

---

[1]   J. S. P. Tatlock and Arthur G. Kennedy, *A Concordance to the Complete Works of Geoffrey Chaucer and to the Romaunt of the Rose* (Washington, 1927).

[2]   References to Chaucer's text here and in the following chapters are to F. N. Robinson (ed.), *The Complete Works of Geoffrey Chaucer*, 2nd ed. (Cambridge, Mass., 1957).

On other occasions they function vitally as pagan semi-deities in the hierarchy of Boethian philosophy (the "Knight's Tale" and *Troilus and Criseyde*).

There are, indeed, several narratives in which Chaucer couples Natura and Fortuna as offstage agents reflecting the conflicts of the characters and thus sets these minor deities in opposition to each other. The purpose of this study is to demonstrate that Chaucer uses the concept of the two allegorical goddesses not only philosophically but also on occasion dramatically, pairing them so that they function in dynamic opposition to each other, with pervasive effect within the narratives.

In an article in 1959, R. M. Lumiansky suggested such a thematic opposition between Natura and Fortuna in the *Book of the Duchess*.[3] Since that article provides a starting point for the present study, I shall summarize it briefly. In this early poem Chaucer sets up the functional opposition in its simplest form: Fortuna equals death and Natura equals life. The two goddesses function dramatically to unify the poem and to contribute to development of the theme of consolation despite bereavement. At the beginning of the poem the grieving Narrator mentions Natura and her relationship to sorrow:

> For sorwful ymagynacioun
> Ys always hooly in my mynde.
> And wel ye woot, agaynes kynde
> Hyt were to lyven in thys wyse;
> For nature wolde nat suffyse
> To noon erthly creature
> Nat longe tyme to endure
> Withoute slep and be in sorwe. (14-21)

Then he proceeds to read a book written "while men loved the lawe of kinde" (56), a book telling of Ceyx' effort to console his wife Alcyone, who nevertheless dies of grief at the loss of her husband. As a result of reading Ceyx' counsel, the Narrator begins to be reconciled to bereavement (224-225) and can find joy

---

[3] "The Bereaved Narrator in Chaucer's *The Book of the Duchess*", *Tulane Studies in English*, IX (1959), 5-17.

in the beauty and bustle of the natural world which he sees in his dream (294-320, 335-343, 344-386, 387-442). He is so much healed that he marvels at the Black Knight's grief, wondering "that Nature / Myght suffre any creature / To have such sorwe, and be not ded" (467-469). Later the Dreamer-Narrator listens to the Black Knight deliver two bitter diatribes against Fortuna (618-649, 805-815). The Black Knight says that the goddess took his Good Fair White from him and is now leading him to grief and death. In rebuttal to the Knight's despair, the Dreamer-Narrator presents the beneficence of Natura as representing life:

> "A, goode sir", quod I, "say not soo!
> Have som pitee on your nature
> That formed yow to creature.
> Remembre yow of Socrates,
> For he ne counted nat thre strees
> Of noght that fortune koude doo."   (710-719)

Through the help of the Dreamer-Narrator the Black Knight realizes that White was Nature's creature, that love is an aspect of Natura, and that excessive grief is violation of Natura's law. Thus, through realization of the vitality of Natura as a cosmic force, first the Narrator and then the Black Knight are led to consolation.

In the three other narratives – the "Physician's Tale", the "Clerk's Tale", the "Knight's Tale" – which we shall later examine in detail, the dramatic opposition between Fortuna and Natura does not operate precisely as in the *Book of the Duchess*. As we shall see, the goddesses are usually antagonistic but interdependent. Usually love can be in the domain of either, with disastrous consequences for the character who chooses the Fortuna-oriented love over the love based on the tenets of Natura. A character does not always, as in the *Book of the Duchess*, choose the tradition of one goddess over that of the other. The Fortuna-equals-death-Natura-equals-life scheme works most readily, though with complications, in the *Troilus* and the *Knight's Tale*, both heavily laden with Boethian thought. Transcending Fortuna is always important in Chaucer. For a character to be defeated by the fickle goddess is for him to die believing that she is supreme; for a character to be victorious over her is for him to die – or live – secure in the philosophical acceptance of God and his agents beyond her. Rising above Fortuna, however, does not mean automatic ascent into a higher realm of Natura. Often Chaucer treats Natura, too, as a sharply limited deity, a view most obvious in the religious tales. Though in her most basic role she is the life-giving principle, Chaucer posits situations in which a character, through a strong act of will or faith, chooses death or acts contrary to the principle of generation, thus conquering not only Fortune but also Nature and achieving a higher spiritual humanity through transcending both, as in the "Physician's Tale" and the "Clerk's Tale".

Before we examine the paired functioning of Fortuna and Natura in the three narratives, a brief sketch of the traditions from which Chaucer draws his concepts is desirable. As scholars have often pointed out, Chaucer uses various sources for his ideas of Fortuna and Natura. The basic notion of the two figures as vying deities comes from Boethius' *De Consolatione Philosophiae*,[4] where the opposition of the goddesses as twin agents of Providence is implicit in Lady Philosophy's discussion in Books I and II. Boethius' concept of Fortuna is often-discussed; references to nature throughout *De Consolatione* are as frequent as those to Fortuna and in Book III more frequent. A point of ambiguity, however, is that Boethius does not consistently consider Nature-as-deity in the same way that he does Fortune. In *De Consolatione* the term nature implies sometimes personification, more often general abstraction. As personification Nature is akin to but less than God: in III. metre 2 she performs a duty – binding the earth in order – already firmly ascribed to God in I. metre 5 and again in III. prose 12 and IV. metre 6. As abstraction Boethius' "nature" is perhaps too general to make concise definition possible. As Boethius discusses with Lady Philosophy the "secretis of nature", of the "nature of things", the term encompasses the constitution and order of the phenomenal universe

---

[4] References to Boethius' *De Consolatione Philosophiae* are to Chaucer's translation, *Boece*.

and of the human being (including involuntary physical processes
– digestion and breathing – as distinct from will and states of
mind and heart), the entire principle of generation and plenitude
(a principle obedient to God and ruled by God's gift of will), the
bond-of-love between all parts of the universe: in short, the
way things are in accord with the way God would have them
("'Thanne is ther nothyng' quod sche, 'that kepith his nature,
that enforceth hym to gon ayen God'" – III. prose 12. 102-104).
Further, in many ways nature is so broadly defined in Boethius
that nature and God are inseparable: "yif blisfulnesse be the
soverayn good of nature that lyveth by resoun, ne thilke thyng
nys nat soverayn good that may ben taken awey in any wise (for
more worthy thyng and more dygne is thilke thyng that mai nat
ben take awey); than scheweth it wel that the unstablenesse of
fortune may nat atayne to resceyven verray blishfulnesse" (II.
prose 4. 142-149). Though in several of nature's general functions, personification may readily be inferred, Boethius clearly
juxtaposes Fortuna and Natura as forces, if not as goddesses.
When Lady Philosophy instructs Boethius to discover his wound
that he may be healed, Boethius replies, "scheweth it nat ynogh
by hymselve the scharpnesse of Fortune, that waxeth wood ayens
me? Ne moeveth it nat the to seen the face or the manere of this
place? . . . Was my face or my chere swych as now whan I soghte
with the the secretis of nature . . . ?'" (I. prose 4. 10-21). The
stroke of Fortuna has negated his life, focused upon following
nature as Lady Philosophy reveals it.
   Lady Philosophy furthers the idea of antagonism between the
two forces as she tells Boethius, "for thow hast foryeten by whiche
governmentz the werld is governed, forthy weenestow that thise
mutacions of fortunes fleten withouten governour. Thise ben
grete causes, noght oonly to maladye, but certes gret causes to
deth. But I thanke the auctour and the makere of hele, that
nature hath nat al forleten the" (I. prose 6. 77-83). Lady Philosophy builds on this basic idea in Book II where, in the role of
the Lady Fortuna, she establishes the polarity between the purposes of the two goddesses from the moment of the birth of the
human being:

Certes I wolde pleten with the a fewe thynges, usynge the woordes of Fortune .... Whan that nature brought the foorth out of thi modir wombe, I resceyved the nakid and nedy of alle thynges, and I norissched the with my richesses, and was redy and ententyf thurw my favour to sustene the – and that maketh the now inpacient ayens me; and I envyrounde the with al the habundaunce and schynynge of alle goodes that ben in my right. Now it liketh me to withdrawe myn hand. Thow hast had grace as he that hath used of foreyne goodes; thow hast no ryght to pleyne the, as though thou haddest outrely forlorn alle thy thynges. Why pleynestow thanne?

(II. prose 2. 1-2, 15-28)

With the skill of loaded diction, Fortuna presents Natura as the villainess and herself as the generous "godmother". She, like Natura, ultimately leaves man "nakid and nedy of alle thynges", but Fortuna does not apply such strong adjectives to the wretched state of man after she has deserted him. Rather, she asks aggrievedly, "Why pleynestow thanne?" Later, Lady Philosophy in her own person demonstrates both the opposition between the two concepts and their paradoxical dependence upon each other:

Fortune ne schal nevere maken that swiche thynges ben thyne that nature of thynges hath maked foreyne fro the. Soth is that, withouten doute, the fruites of the erthe owen to be to the noryssynge of beestis; and yif thow wilt fulfille thyn nede after that it suffiseth to nature, thanne is it no nede that thow seke aftir the superfluyte of fortune. For with ful fewe thynges and with ful litel thynges nature halt hir apayed; and yif thow wolt achoken the fulfillynge of nature with superfluytees, certes thilke thynges that thow wolt thresten or powren into nature schulle ben unjoyeful to the, or elles anoyous.

(II. prose 5. 71-84)

Fortuna showers upon man various worldly favors which are quite opposed to the moderate requirements of Natura, but since man's task is that of realizing that the gifts do not belong permanently to him, the function of Fortuna is actually allied to that of Natura. Here Lady Philosophy observes that since the end is the same for the human being whether or not he depends on Fortuna, reliance on the fickle goddess merely complicates life; the preferable course for man is to realize that "ayenward of litel nedeth hem that mesuren hir fille after the nede of kynde"

(II. prose 5. 121-122). A significant note is that *Le Roman de la Rose* echoes the foregoing ideas, using the personifications of the goddesses rather than the abstractions:

> Ne Fortune ne peut pas faire,
> Tant seit aus omes debonaire,
> Que nules des choses leur seient,
> Coment que conquises les aient,
> Don Nature les fait estranges.[5]

After the powerful discussion of Fortuna which occupies Book II, Book III in turn deals with nature, establishes her as goddess (III. metre 2), and then discusses her as a force belonging to God and representing the qualities mentioned earlier, plenitude, the physical universe, the bond of love. After thorough argument, Boethius through his understanding of the workings of nature is brought to accept Fortuna for the limited and subservient spirit that she ultimately is in *De Consolatione*.

Neither Boethius nor any other one author furnishes the authoritative source for Chaucer's portrayal of either Fortuna or Natura; the references to both goddesses in medieval literature are too extensive to catalogue exhaustively. Chaucer derives the outlines of the personality of Fortuna from Boethius and fills in details of her character from a wealth of popular tradition along with well-established literary sources such as the *Anticlaudianus* of Alain of Lille.[6] Boethius mentions basic qualities of Natura without giving her full dramatic portrayal; hence, Chaucer takes the outline of Natura as dramatic character from Old French tradition and from another of Alain's Latin works, *De Planctu Naturae*.[7] The works of Boethius and Alain are both preliminary,

---

[5] Guillaume de Lorris and Jean de Meun, *Le Roman de la Rose*, II, ed. Ernest Langlois (Paris, 1920), 5315-5319. All references to the *Roman* in this and the following chapters are to this edition. For valuable background reading on Natura in the *Roman*, see Alan F. Gunn, *The Mirror of Love* (Lubbock, 1952).

[6] Alanus de Insulis, *Anticlaudianus*, ed. R. Bossuat (Paris, 1955). References to the *Anticlaudianus* here and in the following chapters are to this edition.

[7] Alanus de Insulis, *Opera Omnia*, in *Patrologia Latina*, CCX, ed. J. P. Migne (Montrouge, 1855), columns 430-482. References to *De Planctu Naturae* here and in the following chapters are to this edition – hereafter

providing impetus for other authors' ideas of the goddesses, and complete, that is, presenting consistent, sustained portraits, Boethius of Fortuna and Alain of Natura.

Just as the occurrences of the goddesses' names are with difficulty catalogued, their traits are with difficulty classified. Several scholars have done monumental research on these female deities, and their works are now standard, H. R. Patch for Fortuna; E. C. Knowlton and, more recently, J. A. W. Bennett for Natura.[8] With reference to them as well as to Boethius and Alain, a superficial summary of the qualities of each goddess is possible. Though the general medieval view of Natura and Fortuna involves a combination of concepts, Christian and pagan, each of the goddesses is surrounded with a nebulous body of tradition. The goddess Fortuna is traditionally fickle, unstable, and irrational, in attributes and appearance composed of extremes of the favorable and the unfavorable.[9] Patch, synthesizing the views of myriad medieval writers, notes that in manner Fortuna is proud, subject to wrath, vindictive, and pitiless.[10] In Christian tradition she is quickly made subordinate to the ruling power of God, and her might is thus subdued. As early as Boethius the arguments are established: Fortuna must be fickle or she would not be Fortuna; since God rules Fortuna, the goddess must ultimately work for good; mischief lies not in Fortuna but in the attitude of the

---

abbreviated *PL*. E. C. Knowlton, "The Goddess Nature in Early Periods", *JEGP*, XIX (1920), 252, establishes this work as a *locus classicus* for Natura down to the sixteenth century. For more recent discussion, see Richard Hamilton Green, "Alain of Lille's *De Planctu Naturae*", *Speculum*, XXXI (1956), 649-674.

[8] Patch, *The Goddess Fortuna in Medieval Literature* (Cambridge, Mass., 1927); Knowlton, "Nature in Early Periods", "Nature in Middle English", *JEGP*, XX (1921), 186-207, "Nature in Old French", *MP*, XX (1922-1923), 309-329, "Nature in Early German", *JEGP*, XXIV (1925), 409-412; Bennett, *The Parlement of Foules: An Interpretation* (Oxford, 1957). Aldo D. Scaglione, *Nature and Love in the Late Middle Ages* (Berkeley, 1963) is valuable for the entire concept of nature in the period. Another vital background work for nature as concept, not as personification, is A. O. Lovejoy, *The Great Chain of Being* (Cambridge, Mass., 1936), especially Chapters III and IV, pp. 67-143.

[9] See Chaucer's *Boece*, Book II. See Alain's *Anticlaudianus*, VIII. 1-62.

[10] Patch, pp. 47, 49.

victim. Dante, in a famous passage in the *Inferno* (VIII. 61-96) unites Christian and pagan traditions by making Fortuna a ministering angel entirely subservient to the Christian God. Logic, however, does not wholly quell Fortuna's irrational effects. She remains, as Patch notes, more frequently unfavorable than favorable. Though in Chaucer as elsewhere she has undeniably Christian connections, often characters in medieval literature who momentarily inveigh against her do not have her underlying consistency in mind but rather focus upon her fickle and irrational pagan face. And in Chaucer, as elsewhere, the characters who briefly invoke her or curse her often take the short view of Fortuna's tumult without relating it to any large Christian purpose: she has caused them woe; they blame her. This response is especially frequent with lovers since one of Fortuna's pastimes is causing trouble for those in love. In brief, besides the extremes and alternations of mood with which the middle ages credit Fortuna, the modern reader can see that in her dramatic appearances she wears another double visage, the Christian and the pagan, often with no more underlying consistency than the emotional state of the character invoking her is capable of at the moment.

Though the two goddesses finally have similar traits, Natura in appearance and characteristics is the antithesis of Fortuna. She is constant, stable, unchanging in temperament, and loving.[11] In Alain's *Anticlaudianus* she is beneficent and beautiful as she presides over the process of creation. In *Le Roman de la Rose* (15900-16012) she continuously works in the forge creating man in order to keep the species ahead of death. Besides her responsibility for generation, hers is the task of giving man the attributes of the common human heritage, as opposed to the worldly favors of Fortuna: [12] "heele of body, strengthe, delivernesse, beautee, gentrice, franchise ... good wit, sharp understondynge, subtil engyn, vertu natureel, good memorie", according to Chaucer's

[11] For a summary of her characteristics, see Alain's *De Planctu*: *PL*, CCX. 293. 35-85.
[12] *Boece*, II. prose 2. 15ff; F. P. Magoun, Jr., "Canterbury Tales A 11", *MLN*, LXXX (1955), 399.

Parson (X. 451-452). In all these duties, one important depth of Natura is her capacity for suffering. As is obvious in the *Roman,* Natura feels anguish at the threat of Death and creatively, though futilely, resists him. More significant, she actively suffers at man's sins against her laws. The whole of *De Planctu Naturae* treats Natura's pain at being violated by man: she appears with her robe cruelly torn (as is Lady Philosophy's in *De Consolatione*) and remains in grief as she speaks to the poet and holds council to decide man's punishment. In this quality of Natura Alain circumvents the doctrine of divine impassibility, that God does not suffer. Asserting that man's wickedness requires divine grief, he relegates the anguish to a minor and originally pagan, but still divine, agent. Natura's pagan origins are perhaps less obtrusive than Fortuna's; usually assimilated into the Christian hierarchy, Natura is repeatedly emphasized as subservient to the beneficent God whom she resembles in the quality of her love. From Boethius to Alain to Jean de Meun to Chaucer, Natura is "the vicaire of the almyghty Lord". Yet the goddess' ready subjection to the Christian God does not resolve all her contradictions. Like Fortuna, she retains pagan overtones – for Natura, chiefly in her function as goddess of generation. As Bennett and Lovejoy observe,[13] the doctrine of Natura's plenitude verges upon heresy. In this doctrine Christian conventions of fidelity and moderation in sexual matters are forgotten. Natura's duty is to see that man increases and multiplies, that he propagates the species; and man, in so doing, partakes of the ultimate creativity of God. At this point the figure of Venus, associated with both Natura and Fortuna, becomes ambiguous. Part of Natura's role is Venus's. The face of Venus which resembles Natura's, however, is not that of the goddess of courtly love convention, but the Venus whom the Wife of Bath's speech and actions invoke (III. 603-611) and whom La Vieille in the *Roman* recalls (12541-14546), the unreflecting vitality of sensual pleasure. The courtly Venus, characterized by artificial formulaic behavior, is consistently associated with Fortuna. True, the flamboyant, unruly side of Natura is

---

[13]   Bennett, pp. 10-11, Lovejoy, p. 84.

usually underplayed in Chaucer, as it is in Alain, and the goddess sometimes seems pallid beside Fortuna, associated as Natura is more with celestial than with worldly matters. But the fecund intensity of the goddess erupts now and again – in Chaucer in such a character as the Wife of Bath or Pandarus, in Jean de Meun in La Vieille or in his conclusion to the *Roman*.

As nearly as one can generalize within the sprawling traditions surrounding Fortuna and Natura, the goddesses are finally both alike and antithetical. Natura works toward love, creativity, life; Fortuna, at least in man's view, toward ill favor or death. Natura is the ally of man, chastising unwillingly and only with great cause; Fortuna acknowledges no allegiance to human beings but holds herself detached, punishing irrationally. Yet even in these antagonistic functions the goddesses are dependent on each other: without Natura's love, Fortuna's aloofness would lose its force; without Natura's creativity, Fortuna could not bring low. In the larger view the goddesses are alike in that both are agents of God's Providence and have the similar task of bringing man – one by positive and the other by negative means – to acknowledge God's sovereignty over human life and to find his own mortal place within the immortal scheme. As noted earlier, in dramatic usage the philosophical purpose is not always foremost, and thus the goddesses' antagonism is often more obvious than their underlying identity. To the modern reader another similarity is obvious: adapted as the goddesses are from pagan origins, both are endowed with overtones of heresy, Natura in the doctrine of plenitude, Fortuna in the possibility of her being regarded an absolute deity, the ultimate irrational cause of human events. Both, even while housed in Christian tradition, in minor ways usurp the sovereignty of God.

Examples are numerous that Natura and Fortuna, rather than being regarded as deities in widely separate spheres of influence, were indeed linked in medieval writings. Knowlton and Patch [14] trace a number of the significant references. Simond de Freine in *Roman de Philosophie*, an Old French redaction of Boethius'

---

[14] Knowlton, "Nature in Old French", pp. 311-314 *et passim*; Patch, pp. 65f, 75f.

De Consolatione, personifies both goddesses and in *Le Songe Veritable* puts Fortuna under Natura in order to show the instability of Fortuna;[15] Eustace Deschamps pictures Natura regretting the subjection of both herself and Fortuna to Amours;[16] Deschamps and others, including Boccaccio, divide God's gifts to man between Fortuna and Natura (and often, Grace, a tradition which Chaucer follows in the "Parson's Tale"), with Natura controlling physical properties both in man and the universe and Fortuna bestowing conditions of worldly weal.[17] Patch further notes that whereas other personifications such as Astrology and the Fates are finally inseparable from Fortuna and are lost in Fortuna's greater identity, a distinction between Fortuna and Natura continues throughout the middle ages.[18] The concept of Natura as deity is powerful enough to withstand the usurping force of Fortuna and to persist with compelling traditions of its own.

The Chaucerian translation from *Le Roman de la Rose*, though probably not entirely the work of Chaucer, includes several typical references to Natura and Fortuna and thus specifically illustrates the qualities of each goddess. Natura is responsible for the setting which surrounds the Rose ("And springyng in a marble ston / Had Nature set, the sothe to telle, / Under that pyn-three a welle" – 1462-1464; "And it hath leves wel foure paire, / That Kynde hath sett, thorough his knowying, / Aboute the rede Rose spryngyng" – 1698-1700). But she is not capable of creating superhuman beauty. Reason's

---

[15] *Oeuvres*, ed. J. E. Matzke (Paris, 1909), 331ff; *Le Songe Veritable*, ed. Maranville (Paris, 1891), 1637-1728 – cited in "Nature in Old French", p. 313.
[16] *Oeuvres Complètes*, ed. Le Saint Hilaire and G. Raynaud (Paris, 1878-1893), V. 307. 21ff – cited in "Nature in Old French", p. 314. See also Guillaume de Machaut, *Dit de l'Alerion, Oeuvres*, ed. Ernest Hoepffner (Paris, 1911), II. 250ff – all references to Machaut's works, unless otherwise specified, are to this edition.
[17] Deschamps, *Oeuvres Complètes*, III, 386; Boccaccio, *De Casibus*, p. 170 – cited in "Nature in Old French", p. 314 and in Patch, p. 66.
[18] Patch, p. 75. He points out (p. 9) that "the history of personified Nature furnishes an interesting parallel for study".

... goodly semblaunt, by devys,
I trowe were maad in paradys;
For Nature hadde nevere such a gras,
To forge a work of such compas.
For certeyn, but if the letter ly,
God himsilf, that is so high,
Made hir aftir his ymage .... (3205-3211)

Further, Natura actively takes delight in love so long as the
ultimate purpose is procreation. Humankind should " ... use
that werk on such a wise / That oon may thurgh another rise. /
Therfore sette Kynde therynne delit .... / Thus hath sotilled
dame Nature" (4863-4865, 4871). But lust is abhorrent to her:
"For of ech synne it is the rote, / Unlefull lust, though it be
sote, / And of all yvell the racyne" (4879-4881).

This view by implication contrasts with Fortuna and the courtly
lover, the root of whose passion is fickle lust – as, for example,
in an earlier reference, "It is of Love, as of Fortune, / That
chaungeth ofte, and nyl contune" (4353-4354). The most striking
references to Fortuna occur in a section which gives full examination to the goddess – her fickleness, as quoted above; her double
aspect (" ... unto men more profit doth / The froward Fortune
and contraire, / Than the swote and debonaire" – 5410-5412);
her variability (" ... she hoteth stabilite / In a stat that is not
stable, / But chaungynge ay and variable" – 5422-5424); and the
negative virtue of her "froward" face ("She makith, thurgh hir
adversite, / Men full clerly for to se / Hym that is freend in
existence / From hym that is by apparence" – 5547-5550). These
briefly summarized statements define many of the major conventions of Fortuna.

Natura assumes importance quite late in the *Roman*, when she
becomes the motivating power for the passion of love. Jean de
Meun dramatizes not only Natura's hatred of death and of abstinence from love (15891-16004) but also her denunciation of
man for his vices and especially for his unnatural lust (19021-
19334). At the end of the *Roman*, Natura both triumphs and is
triumphed against: the courtly lover's winning of the Rose represents the sort of worldly weal bestowed by Fortuna; but the
enthusiastically evocative sexual imagery of the last four hundred

lines recalls the earlier images of Natura at her forge, and the triumph of the lover reaffirms the goddess as the embodiment of plenitude. The Chaucerian version does not include this powerful picture, but the glimpses in the translation show the goddesses in typical attitudes.

Thus the qualities of the goddesses and the shadow of opposition between them is established in the late classical period and continues for centuries. Nor, as noted earlier, is Chaucer the first medieval poet to set the figures in relation to each other. Guillaume de Machaut, contemporary of Chaucer and influence upon his early work, frequently uses both personifications. In a "Ballade" he deals lyrically with the same antagonism which Chaucer later posits dramatically:

> De toutes flours n'avoit et de tous fruis
> en mon vergier fors une seule rose:
> gastes estoit li seurplus et destruis
> par Fortune qui durement s'oppose
>   contre ceste doulce flour
> pour amatir sa coulour et s'odour.
> Mais se cueillir la voy ou trebuchier,
> *autre apres li ja mais avoir ne quier.*
>
> Mais vraiement ymaginer ne puis
> que la vertus, ou ma rose est enclose,
> viengne par toy et par tes faus conduis,
> ains est drois dons natureus; si suppose
>   que tu n'avras ja vigour
> d'amanrir son pris et sa valour.
> Lay la moy donc, qu'ailleurs n'en mon vergier
> *autre apres li ja mais avoir ne quier.*
>
> He! Fortune, qui es gouffres et puis
> pour engloutir tout homme qui croire ose,
> ta fausse loy ou riens de biens ne truis
> ne de seür, trop est decevans chose;
>   ton ris, ta joie, t'onnour
> ne sont que plour, tristesse et deshonnour.
> Se ty faus tour font ma rose sechier,
> *autre apres li ja mais avoir ne quier.*[19]

[19] *Musikalische Werke*, ed. Friedrich Ludwig (Wiesbaden, 1954), pp. 35-36. The edition used for Machaut's other works is cited in note 16, above. Roman numerals refer to volumes.

In Machaut's narratives, besides this brief lyric, both Fortuna
and Natura appear frequently as characters or in allusions. Since
his poems are studded with references to allegorical figures, the
importance of Fortuna and Natura as dynamic forces within the
narratives thus diminishes. Just as in Chaucer, in Machaut neither
goddess necessarily appears: in *Le Dit dou Lyon*, for example,
the major figures are Amours and Dieus. In other narratives
references to the goddesses – more often singly than together –
are frequent. Many appearances of these figures echo conventional motifs. In the *Prologue* Natura offers the poet three of her
children – Scens, Retorique, and Musique – to help him in his
craft (I. 1-127). The *Remede de Fortune* includes many details
of Fortuna's person and habits – her double visage (II. 990,
1161), her buckets (II. 969), her house (II. 1030), her wheel
(II. 1057), her power (sovereign over emperors, popes, and kings
– II. 1179), her chess game (II. 1191) – set within a conventional
love situation. Natura appears in brief glimpses in this poem for
the purpose of endowing a beautiful lady with gifts, of creating
the springtime, and of directing a lover's heart to love the lady.
Machaut points out briefly that Natura, aided by Reason, is
bountiful in a way that Fortuna is not (II. 2468-2473), but does
not develop the contrast. In *Le Dit de L'Alerion* both Fortuna
and Natura appear. Though Natura, who presides over a gather-
ing of birds, is of major importance, the most significant personification is Amours, whom the poet sets above both Fortuna
and Natura (II. 2500). Also in this poem Machaut links Aventure,
Fortuna, and Natura equally (II. 4275-4276). In *Le Jugement
dou Roy de Navarre* Natura figures vitally in the introductory
section: wrathful at man for his evil, she asks Jupiter to send
natural violence – thunder and tempests – upon him (I. 257ff);
later God, sovereign over Natura, sends the plague (I. 347ff).
Machaut portrays the goddess powerfully but changes the tone
abruptly in the love-narrative, focusing on conventional love
themes rather than on Natura, human beings, and a plague-ridden
world. Further, in this same poem he introduces a second image
of Fortuna, Bonneurte (I. 3851 to end), who in Machaut exists
independently of the fickle goddess, though the function of the

two is in many ways the same. Bonneurte, not Fortuna, usurps the interest of the last three hundred lines of the poem: she contains unnumbered good; she controls even Natura (I. 3851-3877). Thus though Fortuna and Natura appear frequently in Machaut's works, they serve, along with the many other personifications, more for narrative decoration or for immediate emphasis of some minor idea (usually having to do with love) than for pervasive thematic purpose. Though Machaut occasionally sets the goddesses in brief opposition, as in the lyric quoted above, he does not, in contrast to Chaucer, through narrative or lyric explore the universe which they represent.

Chaucer's use of the personificatitons of Natura and Fortuna singly and in near-balance – rather than in paired opposition – is worth brief examination. In this discussion I am omitting the short poem "Fortune", and the translations of De Consolatione and the Roman because they are not narratives.[20] The point which I wish to indicate is that with one general exception neither of the deities is ever meaningfully used in total isolation from the other in Chaucer's narratives. When one deity predominates, the other is by implication present, whether or not a conflict between their basic concepts ever develops.

The exception is in the religious narratives. Originally pagan deities though they are, Natura and Fortuna perform their simplest function in the religious tales in the Canterbury collection. In the "Man of Law's Tale", with its framework of the conventional saint's life, and its numerous religious formulae, Fortuna is mentioned by the Man of Law as a member of the Christian hierarchy: "He that is lord of Fortune be thy steere!" (II. 448), he prays, designating Fortuna not as power in her own right but as agent, the pagan deity incorporated as a matter of course into Christian convention. Only one veiled reference to Natura occurs

---

[20] "Fortune", a dialogue between Lady Fortune and "le Pleintif", is a lyric summary of the Boethian view of Fortuna with overtones of the Christian conception formulated by Dante. Chaucer's Boece adds no new concept to the original. I have already used the Romaunt of the Rose in a previous discussion. The section of the poem which contains the most numerous references to Natura and Fortuna is probably not by Chaucer but by a Northern imitator (Robinson, p. 565).

in another religious narrative, the "Prioress' Tale". The slain choirboy says that "by wey of kynde [he] sholde have dyed" (VII. 650-651) but that Christ preserved his life. Though "kynde" here includes the advent of death, popularly outside the authority of Natura, the ultimate power is God's. The reference to "kynde" at this key point emphasizes the supremacy of the Christian deity over any other universal force.

In the Second Nun's invocation to Mary, the Nun prays, "Thow Mayde and Mooder . . . / Thow nobledest so ferforth oure nature, / That no desdeyn the Makere hadde of kynde / His Sone in blood and flessh to clothe and wynde" (VIII. 36, 40-42). Mary elevates the character and potentiality, the "nature", of man so that God does not hesitate to send his Son to humankind. Here man's nature, properly the province of Natura, is usurped by Mary for God's divine purpose. In this detail the Second Nun's reference negates any shadow of identification between Natura and the Virgin Mary, a correspondence which apparently had existed – for example, Bernardus Sylvestris applies to Natura the phrase *gratiae plena*[21] – as the religious teller raises the key figures in the Christian hierarchy above any other cosmic force. Within the body of the tale itself, Tiburce, suffused with the odor of sanctity, observes, "The sweete smel that in myn herte I fynde / Hath chaunged me al in another kynde" (VIII. 251-252). Once more the power of the Christian miracle works change in the basic qualities of body and soul traditionally in Natura's care.

In the "Parson's Tale" Natura and Fortuna both appear, as noted earlier, in a triumvirate with the Christian concept of grace – here again, the matter-of-fact inclusion of originally pagan elements into the Christian background to suit immediate didactic requirements:

Now myghte men axe wherof that Pride sourdeth and spryngeth, and I seye, somtyme it spryngeth of the goodes of nature, and somtyme of the goodes of fortune, and somtyme of the goodes of grace. / Certes, the goodes of nature stonden outher in goodes of body or in

---

[21] From *De Mundo Universitate*, quoted in Bennett, p. 108. See also Alain's *Anticlaudianus,* I. 52 and IV. 88, where the poet refers to Natura as "Gracia Nature".

goodes of soule. / . . . Goodes of fortune been richesse, hyghe degrees
of lordshipes, preisynges of the peple. / Goodes of grace been science,
power to suffre spiritueel travaille, benignitee, vertuous contem-
placioun, withstondynge of temptacioun, and symblable thynges. / Of
whiche forseyde goodes, certes it is a ful greet folye a man to priden
hym in any of hem alle.   (X. 449-455)

Whether the terms used here represent the abstractions or the
personifications is immaterial, since the attribute of gift-giving
associates Natura and Fortuna by analogy with the personifications of the goddesses in Alain's *Anticlaudianus*, where the allegorical personifications present gifts to the newly created human
being.[22] The Parson also discusses how the gifts of these three
embody possibility for the sin of pride. Caution against the favors
of Fortuna becomes standard with *De Consolatione*, but warnings
against the gifts of Natura are an innovation, since Natura's usual
role is that of constant and loving benefactress. The Parson's
admonition against Natura's "goodes" of body and of soul is
lengthy and detailed. He gives treatment to the goods of Fortuna
and of Grace, but in much briefer fashion. Thus he pulls the pagan
figures directly into the Christian framework, leaving them, in
the process of admonition, something less than deities.

The tales of the other professionally religious pilgrims – the
Friar, the Monk, and the Nun's Priest – are outside the conventionally Christian stream. But it is significant that of those
who emphasize the Christian theme, all refer directly or indirectly
to one of the deities (the Parson is the only teller who mentions
both Fortuna and Natura) and – less surprisingly – all subordinate
the deities to the Christian God. Of importance probably is the
fact that in three of the tales the pagan figure thus "put down"
is Natura. As her beneficent glory wanes, the beneficent power
of God appears the brighter. I am aware that evidence for gen-
eralization is extremely limited. There are, however, indications
of a pattern in these four tales: use of both Fortuna and Natura
gives the deities associations with each other, associations with
non-Christian overtones; use of one figure (the tales of the Man
of Law, the Prioress, and the Second Nun) or of three (the "Par-

---

[22]   *Anticlaudianus*, VII. 117-396.

son's Tale") squelches possibility for conflict between the goddesses. The supremacy of God, not the note of contention between
figures in the hierarchy, is what these speakers stress.

Though scholars have not found the unfinished *Anelida and
Arcite* especially exciting,[23] the fragment contains undertones of
Fortuna-Natura conflict. The figures of the goddesses are put
before the eyes of the reader early in the poem, within thirty-five
lines of each other. The description of Theseus the conqueror
riding toward Athens "in al the flour of Fortunes yevynge" (44)
is one of the first concrete pictures in the narrative and casts a
background image throughout the poem, an image the more
striking since Theseus, with this reference, rides straight out of
the poem and no further reference to him appears. Anelida the
queen of Ermony is next introduced:

> Yong was this quene, of twenty yer of elde,
> Of mydel stature, and of such fairenesse,
> That Nature had a joye her to behelde;
> And for to speken of her stidfastnesse,
> She passed hath Penelope and Lucresse;
> And shortly, yf she shal be comprehended,
> In her ne myghte no thing been amended.   (78-84)

In the next stanza Arcite is presented in terms which echo the
quintessential characteristics of Fortuna: "But he was double in
love and no thing pleyn, / And subtil in that craft over any
wyght. / . . . But he was fals" (87-88, 97). Thus the reference to
Anelida as a creature of Natura is framed emphatically by references, either direct or indirect, to Fortuna.

The love affair of Anelida and Arcite turns upon Arcite's
"newfanglenesse", for he is soon smitten with another lady, who
is as fickle a taskmistress as the fickle Fortuna: "Her daunger
made him bothe bowe and bende, / And as her liste, made him
turne or wende; / . . . She sente him now to londe, now to shippe;
/ And for she yaf him daunger al his fille, / Therfor she hadde

[23]   Madeleine Fabin, "On Chaucer's *Anelida and Arcite*", *MLN*, XXXIV
(1919), 269, compares Chaucer's fragment with a similar *lai* of Machaut.
She observes that Machaut is more optimistic than Chaucer because he
has both "destinee" and "Diex" at his service; Chaucer, who has only
Fortune, is the more despondent.

him at her owne wille" (186-187, 194-196). Arcite's consummate
trick is in attempting to "cover his traitorie" by swearing that
Anelida was false to him. Anelida, because of Arcite's "kun-
nyng" in assuring her "trouthe", makes the mistake which mortals usually do with Fortuna's gifts: "she him trusted over any
creature" (91). As the result of her trust, she is prey to his further
double-dealing as he commands her wilfully, feigns jealousy, and
finally "falses" her. Anelida's reaction to his treachery is significant: she responds with the typical pattern of the forsaken
courtly lover whose extravagant grief arises from the lover's
having relied on the whim of Fortuna for granting and snatching
away love: [24]

> She wepith, waileth, swowneth pitously;
> To grounde ded she falleth as a ston;
> Craumpyssheth her lymes crokedly;
> She speketh as her wit were al agon;
> Other colour then asshen hath she noon;
> Non other word speketh she, moche or lyte,
> But "merci, cruel herte myne, Arcite!"   (169-175)

She "Pyneth day be day in langwisshinge" (205) before "ful
sorowfully wepinge" (207) she writes a complaint containing all
the clichés of the forsaken lover (in fact, her attitude, including
her epistle, resembles nothing in Chaucer so much as the "kan-
kedort" typical of the forlorn Troilus). The fragment ends with
her sacrificing to Mars, a deity associated with the inconstant
aspect of Venus (because of Vulcan's catching them making love)
and hence with Fortuna. [25]

A contrast of the *Anelida and Arcite* with the *Legend of Good
Women* presents itself at this point. In none of the nine tragedies

---

[24] Cf. *Troilus and Criseyde*, I. 836-840; the "Knight's Tale", I. 1355-
1371. For Ovid's list of the desolate lover's characteristics, see Thomas
A. Kirby, *Chaucer's Troilus: A Study in Courtly Love* (Baton Rouge,
1940), pp. 7-12.
[25] Cf. Arcite's prayer to Mars in the "Knight's Tale", I. 2382-2392. The
Mars-Venus-Vulcan episode is itself ambiguous, linked in some ways with
both Fortuna and Natura. In the *Roman* (13847ff), La Vieille chides
Vulcan for interfering with the amoral exuberance of Natura's plenitude.
But here and in the "Knight's Tale" Chaucer sets the episode within the
context of false courtly love, in the dominion of Fortuna.

of the *Legend* does Chaucer depict the lady in the excess of emotion in which he lengthily describes Anelida. The scenes of grief in the *Legend* are by comparison restrained, and on occasion Chaucer even goes out of his way to avoid making them specific. The episode of Dido and Aeneas, for example, is the one which, in treatment, bears most resemblance to *Anelida and Arcite*. Dido, on discovering that Aeneas is leaving,

> ... kneleth, cryeth, that routhe is to devyse;
> Conjureth hym, and profereth hym to be
> His thral, his servant in the leste degre;
> She falleth hym to fote and swouneth ther,
> Dischevele, with hire bryghte gilte her,
> And seyth, "Have mercy! and let me with yow ryde!"
>   (1311-1316)

But she does speak rationally (as Anelida does not), and she has a sound reason for wishing Aeneas to stay: "I am with child, and yeve my child his lyf!" (1323). Chaucer mentions her swooning "twenty tyme", but he leaves vague her outpouring of grief, "of which I may nat wryte, / So gret a routhe I have it for t'endite" (1344-1345). And he gives scant treatment to her piteous letter to Aeneas: "But who wol al this letter have in mynde, / Rede Ovyde, and in hym he shall it fynde" (1366-1367). Likewise, of Hipsipyle's letter of complaint Chaucer says only, "A letter sente she to hym, certeyn, / Which were to longe to wryten and to sen" (1564-1565). Medea's epistle he dismisses similarly (1678-1679) and also Ariadne's (2218-2220). There is a thematic possibility for Chaucer's vagueness besides the dramatically sound reason of avoiding monotony and maudlinity. With emphasis on their suffering and swooning, the ladies' behavior would resemble the inordinate grief of the courtly lover; [26] and Chaucer's point with the *Legend* is that the ladies are the

[26] A striking example of Chaucer's unwillingness to overemphasize grief occurs in the *Troilus*. When Criseyde hears that she is to be traded to the Greeks, she is in anguish. Chaucer treats her woe thus:

> If I discryven wolde hire hevynesse,
> It sholde make hire sorwe seme lesse
> Than that it was, and childisshly deface
> Hire heigh compleynte, and therefore ich it pace.
>   (IV. 802-805)

constant ones, steadfast members of the troupe of Alceste. The springtime setting, Alceste's garb of green and white, and her role in the "Prologue" lend the queen associations with Natura; hence, it is not surprising that she requests tales of women who with long-suffering bear the fickleness and treachery of the men. Anelida is the same type of character as the ladies in the *Legend*, but Chaucer gives her entirely different reactions. The fragment of the poem which exists indicates that he is creating for dramatic and philosophical purposes a topsy-turvy system of values. Beguiled by a willing vassal of Fortuna, Anelida, Natura's creature, succumbs to a Fortuna-dominated universe where "hit is kynde of man" (149) to be false and where "the kynde of mannes herte is to delyte / In thing that straunge is" (201-202); and she acts in accord with the philosophical temper that surrounds her, even assuming what is traditionally the lover's role, not the mistress', in her grief. The fragment ends with Natura's creature undone and wretched because of her trust in false values and the fickle state of worldly weal. There is no clue to later events and philosophical attitudes, but ample signs of the Fortuna-theme and perhaps of a Fortuna-Natura conflict pervade the early part of the poem.

The subject of Fortune in the "Monk's Tale" is oft-discussed, and I am giving the tale scant treatment here.[27] My purpose in mentioning the tale at all is to suggest that even in this Fortuna-centered narrative the presence of the one influence assumes the presence of the other. The shadow of Fortuna appears immediately in the tale, with the Monk's announcement, "For certein, whan that Fortune list to flee, / Ther may no man the cours of hire withholde" (VII. 1995-1996), and in the earlier tragedies he feels called upon to explain her absence. There is no mention of Natura in the tale and Fortuna certainly emerges triumphant; thus, there is no possibility for dynamic conflict between the goddesses. Even in this Fortune-ruled world of medieval tragedy, however, the power of goddesses is interdependent. Several of the characters pervert the realm of Natura or use Natura for

[27] For an original treatment, see Edward M. Socola, "Chaucer's Development of Fortune in the 'Monk's Tale'", *JEGP*, XLIX (1950), 159-171.

their own purposes and are thus brought low. For misgovernance of Eden, natural paradise, Adam is driven out into a world of chaos (VII. 2012-2014). Nebuchadnezzar, for his pride, is cast to the level of a wild beast, in total perversion of human dignity, until he regains humility (VII. 2177ff). Nero, too, commits crimes against Natura: he slays his brother, lies with his sister, and "his mooder made he in pitous array, / For he hire wombe slitte to biholde / Where he conceyved was; so weilaway! / That he so litel of his mooder tolde" (VII. 2483-2486); thus, Fortuna gleefully brings him low. Antiochus, prideful because of Fortuna's favors, gains exalted notions of his powers over Natura and meets his doom diseased with worms (VII. 2583ff). Hercules' Dianira seems "fressh as May" (VII. 2120) but gives Hercules a poisoned robe, the instrument through which, because of his trust in Dianira, he meets his downfall: "Lo, who may trust on Fortune any throwe?" (VII. 2136). No clear pattern works out for all of the examples, but shadows of a Fortuna-Natura counter-influence underlie a number of the Monk's tragedies.

The "Monk's Tale", involved as it is with a series of examples, does not portray Fortuna as deeply affecting a dramatic situation; *Troilus and Criseyde* does. Almost no scholar has written on the *Troilus* without considering Fortuna.[28] Up to a point this brief

[28] The most complete study of Fortuna in the poem is Walter Clyde Curry, "Destiny in Chaucer's *Troilus*", *PMLA*, XLV (1930), 129-168. Since I am giving the poem only secondary treatment, I am not attempting to summarize the prodigious amount of scholarship on the *Troilus*. Helpful works include Morton W. Bloomfield, "Distance and Predestination in *Troilus and Criseyde*", *PMLA*, LXXII (1957), 14-26; Alfred David, "The Hero of the *Troilus*", *Speculum*, XXXVII (1962), 566-581; T. P. Dunning, "God and Man in *Troilus and Criseyde*", *English and Medieval Studies*, ed. Norman Davis and C. L. Wrenn (London, 1962), pp. 164-182; Robert M. Jordan, "The Narrator in Chaucer's *Troilus*", *ELH*, XXV (1958), 237-257; C. S. Lewis, "What Chaucer really did to *Il Filostrato*", *Essays and Studies*, XVII (1932), 56-75; R. M. Lumiansky, "The Function of the Proverbial Monitory Elements in Chaucer's *Troilus and Criseyde*", *Tulane Studies in English*, II (1950), 5-48; Robert D. Mayo, "The Trojan Background of the *Troilus*", *ELH*, IX (1942), 245-256; H. R. Patch, "Troilus on Determinism", *Speculum*, VI (1931), 225-243, and "Troilus on Predestination", *JEGP*, XVII (1918), 399-422; D. W. Robertson, "Chaucerian Tragedy", *ELH*, XIX (1952), 1-37; James L. Shanley, "The

discussion supports the analyses of Alfred David and T. P. Dunning.[29] These view Troilus as groping for and (as the speech from the eighth sphere and the Narrator's epilogue indicate) in a measure achieving in his pagan world, through the depth of his love for Criseyde, the fulfillment which comes through love of God. The roles of Fortuna and Natura are ambiguous, working on two levels: they embody the notion of subordination to God, as expressed in the religious tales, and yet they represent the alternative ways – the only possible choices for the pagans in the poem – of viewing and reacting to the universe. The influence of the one deity again assumes the influence of the other; the *Troilus* counters the force of Fortuna with that of Natura.

A reading of the text indicates the unlikelihood of a dynamic opposition between Fortuna and Natura. Throughout the poem the fickle goddess Fortuna is mentioned twenty-four times; and the goddess of Kind, three, with several other significant references to the general realm of "nature" or "kind".[30] Though certain characters are preoccupied with Fortuna, no other characters tip the balance through preoccupation with Natura, and no character shows much of a wavering between the poles of the two goddesses. One significant point is that Narrator and characters view Fortuna differently. To the characters she is an absolute goddess; to the Narrator she is agent not Cause, not absolute but obedient to God (III. 617ff, V. 1541-1547). The equations are not perfect. There is much Boethian "talk" in the poem – laments and questions from Troilus, answers from Pandarus. But Chaucer's point here seems ironic. Though Troilus in love may be

---

Troilus and Christian Love", *ELH*, VI (1939), 271-281. Since I am treating the *Troilus* only briefly, I do not mention its relationship to Boccaccio's *Il Filostrato*.

[29] David, "The Hero of the *Troilus*", Dunning, "God and Man in *Troilus and Criseyde*". See also Shanley, "The Troilus and Christian Love".

[30] References to personified Fortuna: Book I–138, 837, 841, 843, 849; III–617, 1667, 1714; IV–2, 260, 274, 324, 385, 600, 1189, 1192, 1588, 1682; V–469, 1134, 1460, 1541, 1745, 1763. General references to the goddess: II–285, 335; IV–391. References to personified Natura: II–1374; IV–251, 1096. Other general references to Natura's realm: I–238, 979; III–1016, 1437, 1730, 1765; IV–451, 1096; V–209, 829.

analogous in misery to the imprisoned Boethius, Pandarus is no
Lady Philosophy.[31] Pandarus' every answer involves the handy
platitude; his easy dicta on Fortuna (I. 841ff, II. 281ff, III.
1625ff, IV. 384ff) are commonplaces, not urgent argument, and
Chaucer in his winning portrayal of Pandarus' loquacity treats
them as such. Pandarus, Criseyde, and Troilus in his bewilder-
ment see no relation between Fortuna and a valid basis for human
action. To them, despite the platitudes, she remains the irrational,
inexplicable goddess. To the Narrator the concept of Fortuna
makes more sense. With his distanced perspective he relegates
the goddess beneath the hand of God, and thus his view of the
lovers' plight is more complex, balanced, and thoughtful than
their own. Though he, not Pandarus, is analogous to Lady
Philosophy, he cannot speak to the actors in the drama. Again
the equation is not exact; the poem is far too complex for easy
patterning. The Narrator's comments include occasional tag
references to Fortuna invoking the goddess' own authority. These,
however, do not preclude the ultimate authority of God – even
Fortuna has free latitude for operation – and further they re-
inforce the Narrator's sympathetic attempt to see the tragedy
from his characters' perspective. Natura, on the contrary, when
invoked – as rarely happens – by characters or Narrator, is placed
in a subordinate station: "O thow Jove, O auctour of nature!"
(III. 1016); " ... God, maker of kynde ... " (III. 1437); "So
wolde God, that auctour is of kynde, / That with his bond Love
of his vertu liste / To cerclen hertes alle, and faste bynde ... "
(III. 1765-1767). She is accorded reverence and holy sanction,
and yet she is not a directly moving force. Her amoral pagan
energy erupts, as will be mentioned later, in two of the characters,
Pandarus and Criseyde, but plays no vital part in the major
theme. On the whole, the pagans, looking at Natura, sense divine
force beyond her but are willess and powerless to relate to it;
when viewing Fortuna, they consider her absolute. Their philo-

---

[31] For a fuller treatment, in a slightly different direction, of Pandarus'
role as a parody of Lady Philosophy's, see Alan Gaylord, "Uncle Pandarus
as Lady Philosophy", *Papers of the Michigan Academy of Science, Arts,
and Letters*, XLVI (1960), 571-595.

sophical and spiritual vision is split. The Narrator's, within the Christian framework, is more consistent.

The influence of Natura expresses itself most strongly in the crescendoing grace of the love affair, focused in the person of Troilus. Through his intuitive grasp of natural law and of the presence of God behind the goddess' manifestations, Troilus reaches transcendent understanding briefly in his earthly life and again after death. Though the scene in the *Troilus* is not consistently one of natural beauty or of springtime (in contrast with the "Knight's Tale"), Chaucer repeatedly links the love affair with natural fecundity and beauty; in crises of the affair he expresses the lovers' emotions – and especially Troilus' – through extended similes from nature (II. 764-770; II. 967-973; III. 351-357, 1233-1239; IV. 225-231, 239-245, 1432-1435). Both Pandarus (II. 1374) and Criseyde (III. 1016, 1437) mention the goddess and her natural realm.[32] The minor character Antigone, in addition, seems to exist for no other reason than to serve as a handmaiden of love-according-to-Natura: "Antigone the shene" (II. 824), "fresshe Antigone the white" (II. 887) stands in the May garden and sings to love a song of dedication so moving that Criseyde asks, "Lord, is ther swych blisse among / Thise loveres, as they konne faire endite?" (II. 885-886). Antigone then lectures her on the difference between courtly love and love in accordance with Natura:

> "Ye, wis . . .
> For alle the folk that han or ben on lyve
> Ne konne wel the blisse of love discryve.
>
> "But wene ye that every wrecche woot
> The parfite blisse of love? Why, nay, iwys!
> They wenen all be love, if oon be hoot.
> Do wey, do wey, they woot no thyng of this!"   (II. 887-893)

Her accents are deepened and universalized by Troilus as the affair approaches consummation, and his instinctive grasp of the

---

[32] Robert apRoberts, "The Central Episode in Chaucer's *Troilus*", *PMLA*, LXXVII (1962), 378, discusses the influence of natural forces – the smoky rain – on Criseyde's yielding.

holy bond of love from creature to Creator, the highest realm
to which Natura can lead the human spirit, bursts forth:

> ". . . O Love, O Charite!
> . . . .
> Benigne Love, thow holy bond of thynges . . . .
> Yet were al lost, that dar I wel seyn certes,
> But if thi grace passed oure desertes."
>
> (III. 1254, 1261, 1266-1267)

> "Love, that of erthe and se hath governaunce,
> Love, that his hestes hath in hevenes hye,
> Love, that with an wholesome alliaunce
> Halt peples joyned, as hym lest hym gye,
> Love, that knetteth lawe of compaignie,
> And couples doth in vertu for to dwelle,
> Bynd this acord, that I have told and telle."   (III. 1744-1750)

Chaucer has earlier emphasized that Troilus' love surpasses mere
lyrical precept; he is ennobled to selfless and super-knightly
behavior.

Through love, in accord with the holiest mandates of Natura,
Troilus reaches abstract, universal understanding. Through the
influence of Fortuna, as he believes, he falls from weal to
woe and thus from understanding to despair, from abstract
selflessness to concrete self-absorption. The Narrator, outside
in time, sees God behind both earthly love and earthly loss,
but Troilus finally cannot make the spiritual leap from lesser
agents to Creator and Cause. To focus Troilus' forthcoming
dilemma more forcefully, the Narrator speaks in terms of Fortuna, not of God, though the Narrator's Fortuna is that of the
enlightened Boethius, not that of the incompletely understanding
Troilus. Between Troilus' two lyrical outcries lauding holy love,
the Narrator twice calls notice to the truth, unseen by Troilus,
that the happiness of the lovers is dependent on Fortuna (III.
1667-1668, III. 1714-1715). The tension builds through dramatic irony: the holy state in which Troilus momentarily dwells is
juxtaposed against the state of uncertain weal which the Narrator
knows is the context of mortal life.

When the truth of Troilus' felicity is put to the test with the
word that Criseyde has been traded to the Greeks, he immediately

betrays his transcendent peace as he reacts personally, automatically, and unreflectingly: after cursing his birth at the hand
of Natura (IV. 250-252), he lengthily rails at Fortuna as the
culprit (IV. 260-329). From this point on he thinks and acts
increasingly in terms of his own concrete misery. His last attempt
to reason with issues outside himself comes with his speech on
predestination, and here his resolutions mirror his growing despair as he reaches the thoughtful but emotionally flat conclusion
that " . . . thus the bifallyng / Of thynges that ben wist bifore the
tyde, / They mowe nat ben eschued on no syde" (IV. 1076-
1078). As Criseyde's departure becomes imminent and at last
occurs, Troilus' contact with any abstract force becomes increasingly brief and bitter. "O cruel Jove, and thow, Fortune
adverse, / . . . Fy on youre myght and werkes so dyverse!" (IV.
1192, 1195), he accuses when he thinks Criseyde is dead. This
is his last mention of Fortuna in the poem. In all his woe that
follows, Troilus does not invoke or blame the fickle lady. Indeed,
except for a brief but intense imprecation against every deity he
can think of (including the realm of nature) immediately after he
has turned Criseyde over to Diomedes (V. 205-210), he has had
done with supernatural forces. His thoughts throughout the rest
of the poem ascend no higher than over the city wall to the
Greek camp. One of his laments ironically takes the form of the
ubi sunt complaint, but his dirge does not use beauty or bravery
as an excuse for asking "ou sont les neiges d'antan?" Instead, in
the intensity of his despair he can think only of his own loss and
makes no attempt to universalize it:

> "Wher is myn owene lady, lief and deere?
> Wher is hire white brest? wher is it, where?
> Wher ben hire armes and hire eyen cleere,
> That yesternyght this tyme with me were?"   (V. 218-221)

and later when he sees the brooch which proves Criseyde's infidelity:

> ". . . O lady myn, Criseyde,
> Where is youre feith, and where is youre biheste?
> Where is your love? where is youre trouthe?" he seyde.
> "Of Diomede have ye now al this feeste!"   (V. 1674-1677)

With the question of lovers' faith constantly hanging throughout
the last two books of the poem, Troilus' desperate query of course
assumes overtones of the universal, but the point is that in the
last part of the poem the universality comes from the almost
unbearable poignance; the philosophical tensions lie in the background.

When Troilus has the dream of the boar embracing Criseyde,
he must call on Cassandra the prophetess to make the link between concrete vision and abstract meaning. She, to prepare
him for the woeful news, calls to his mind the dominance of
Fortuna over human affairs ("Thow most a fewe of olde stories
heere, / To purpos, how that Fortune overthrowe / Hath lordes
olde" – V. 1459-1461) and puts her point across unmistakably
by telling example after example. When she finally explicates
his dream, she does so in specific, one-syllable words ("This
Diomede hire herte hath, and she his. / Wep if thow wolt, or lef!
For out of doute, / This Diomede is inne, and thow art oute" –
V. 1517-1519). After Criseyde's infidelity is unquestionable,
Troilus translates his self-absorption in terms of action, not
philosophy: he wants to meet Diomedes in hand-to-hand combat
and he wants to die himself, and he spends the remainder of
his days in battle until he is slain by Achilles. Thus, as the
intensity of his personal woe increases, the circle of his awareness
becomes sharply limited; he cannot see past himself to universal
rule or misrule. After death, when he is freed from self he again
achieves in purer form the transcendent knowledge that he had
glimpsed on earth.

Though Troilus ceases to refer to Fortuna in Book IV, the
name of the goddess does not disappear from the poem. Chaucer
keeps her influence obvious through the Narrator, who mentions
her power over Troilus and the city fully six times in the last
book.[33] Again the references function on a double level – Fortuna
is at once the irrational goddess upon which Troilus blames his
downfall and the providential agent of God which the Narrator
acknowledges. During this period when Troilus is too self-pre-
occupied to be concerned with universal concepts, the Narrator's

[33]   Lines 469, 1134, 1460, 1541, 1745, 1763.

references to Fortuna emphasize her disastrous effect. During the course of the final book the Narrator broadens the "infortune" of the goddess to include both Troilus' private woe and the public doom of Troy: "Fortune ... / Gan pulle awey the fetheres brighte of Troie / Fro day to day, til they ben bare of joie" (V. 1541, 1546-1547). Then in the last lines he hammers home the inevitability of Fortuna's doom to Troilus and the city:

> Gret was the sorwe and pleynte of Troilus;
> But forth hire cours Fortune ay gan to holde ....
> Swich is this world, whoso it kan byholde:
> In ech estat is litel hertes reste.
> God leve us for to take it for the beste!
>
> (V. 1744-1745, 1747-1750)

In the last book the Narrator, in presenting Fortuna on Troilus' terms, shows the effect of regarding the goddess as absolute; since Troilus and Troy acknowledge her sway, devastation is inevitable and nothing, not even human self-respect, can be salvaged.

The other important characters do not contribute to any total pattern of conflict between Natura and Fortuna. Criseyde perhaps typifies the result of the pagans' incomplete philosophical pattern in that she bases her actions on immediate necessity rather than on any metaphysical standard and proceeds as best she can with the task of living. In some ways she seems allied with the goddess of Kind (she is much a part of the ritualistic springtime scene in the garden – II. 813ff; she falls deeply in love; she is undone at the thought of leaving her love – IV. 743ff); in some ways, with Fortuna (Criseyde possesses the goddess' basic characteristic, instability). In her unfaithfulness to Troilus, she seems to partake of qualities of both. Like Fortuna, in her infidelity she provides to Troilus tangible proof of the uncertainty of worldly weal. Like Natura, she must love – if not Troilus, then Diomedes. In this compulsion Criseyde shares in the irrational vitality of generative Natura, the pagan figure acknowledging no authority but her own impulses. Chaucer presents her intensely human qualities in intensely human fashion, unreconciled.

Pandarus, too, echoes the amoral, fecund voice of the goddess Natura. He can deliver sound rhetoric on Fortuna and he can philosophize when the occasion demands, but he is more concerned with the immediate joys of springtime and of love. His most characteristic remarks are, "Do wey youre book, rys up, and lat us daunce, / And lat us don to May some observaunce" (II. 111-112); "... as thow wel woost thiselve, / This town is ful of ladys al aboute; / ... If she be lost, we shal recovere an other" (IV. 400-401, 406); "Hath Kynde the wrought al only hire to plese?" (IV. 1096). On the whole, the goddesses Natura and Fortuna increase the philosophical and dramatic tensions in the Troilus, though they do not, as a pair, become vitally moving forces.

In the *Parliament of Fowls* Natura but not Fortuna enters directly as a character. The poem has been much in critical vogue,[34] and this discussion does not purport to reinterpret it completely. Certainly the *Parliament* is helpful for revealing Natura as Chaucer views her and for pointing out an idea which, as we shall see, Chaucer develops in the "Clerk's Tale" and the "Knight's Tale": that the code of courtly love, as associated with Venus, is not in accord with the credo of Natura. Though Natura's associations with Christian *caritas* are unmistakable – she is, after all, "vicaire of the almyghty Lord" and Chaucer refers to her as "ful of grace" – these paragraphs do not define the

[34] For background, see Bennett. For a summary of criticism see Donald C. Baker, "The Poet of Love and the *Parlement of Foules*", *University of Mississippi Studies in English*, II (1961), 78-110. Other useful works are Dorothy Bethurum, "Chaucer's Point of View as Narrator in the Love Poems", *PMLA*, LXXIV (1959), 511-520; Robert W. Frank, Jr., "Structure and Meaning in the *Parlement of Foules*", *PMLA*, LXXI (1956), 530-539; Bernard F. Huppé and D. W. Robertson, *Fruyt and Chaf: Studies in Chaucer's Allegories* (Princeton, 1963), pp. 101-148; R. M. Lumiansky, "Chaucer's *Parlement of Foules*: A Philosophical Interpretation", *RES*, XXIV (1948), 81-89; Charles O. McDonald, "An Interpretation of Chaucer's *Parlement of Foules*", *Speculum*, XXX (1955), 444-457; Charles A. Owen, Jr., "The Role of the Narrator in the *Parlement of Foules*", *CE*, XIV (1953), 264-269; Gardiner Stillwell, "Unity and Comedy in Chaucer's *Parlement of Foules*", *JEGP*, XLIX (1950), 470-495, and "Chaucer's Eagles and Their Choice on February 14", *JEGP*, LIII (1954), 546-561.

meaning of the poem as Christian exegesis. Chaucer's narrative power in the poem encompasses the unspoken pagan depths of Natura which make her paradoxically akin and hostile to the courtly Venus.[35]

The difference between the gardens of Venus and of Natura is that between the static and the organic. Though Venus and her setting are not associated directly with Fortuna, the warning on the gate gives indication that part of the kingdom within does not spring from Natura's beneficence and is, indeed, suggestive of death:

> "Thorgh me men gon", than spak that other side,
> "Unto the mortal strokes of the spere
> Of which Disdayn and Daunger is the gyde,
> There nevere tre shal fruyt ne leves bere.
> This strem yow ledeth to the sorweful were
> There as the fish in prysoun is al drye;
> Th'eschewing is only the remedye!"   (134-140)

The description of the park itself begins with a pleasing note of naturalness which seemingly belies the legend on the gate. Immediately after the Dreamer-Narrator is shoved inside, everywhere he looks is suffused with natural beauty. He sees trees "of colour fresh and greene" (174), a "gardyn ... ful of blosmy bowes" (183), a "ryver" and a "grene mede" (184), "floures white, blewe, yelwe, and rede" (186), and "colde welle-stremes, nothyng dede, / That swymmen ful of smale fishes lighte" (187-188). All that the Narrator sees from close inside the gate is suggestive of life:

> On every bow the bryddes herde I synge,
> With voys of aungel in here armonye;
> Some besyede hem here bryddes forth to brynge;
> The litel conyes to here pley gonne hye;
> And ferther al aboute I gan aspye
> The dredful ro, the buk, the hert and hynde,
> Squyrels, and bestes smale of gentil kynde.   (190-196)

The place seems the quintessence of natural beauty. As the

---

[35] For an interpretation of the poem as Christian allegory, see Huppé and Robertson, pp. 101-148.

Narrator leaves this first region of the park (which, as he later
reveals – 295-301 – is where Natura sits), the atmosphere
changes, though he seems not fully aware of the change. His
vision is naive; he is still enchanted with the appearance of the
park from the gate, even as he enters farther into Venus' garden.
The most telling evidence of this naivete is that his general observation of "joye more a thousandfold / Than man can telle"
(208-209) never materializes into the concrete images which in
Chaucer convey the final truth. A definite note of foreboding
enters with the first sight that he sees – Cupid and his daughter
Will, the only two figures engaged in meaningful activity. They
are busily preparing Cupid's arrows, "Some for to sle, and some
to wounde and kerve" (217). As he nears the temple he sees
frenzied motion (the women dancing about the temple – 232-
235) and ponderous repose (Dames Pees and Pacience – 240-244),
and as he enters he hears the sighs of the jealous lovers (246-
252). Inside the temple he sees Venus herself, who is associated
with the static perfection which characterizes the park: she lies
at ease on her couch of gold awaiting the sunset which will never
come to this place of perpetual daylight and listens to the cries
of the eternally supplicating pair of lovers (278-279). None of
the sights nor sounds is connotative of joy; everything is static,
unchanging, antidynamic. The final dimension of stasis – death –
is suggested as the Dreamer-Narrator walks to the recesses of
the temple and sees the list of lovers and their legends:

> Semyramis, Candace, and Hercules,
> Biblis, Dido, Thisbe, and Piramus,
> Tristam, Isaude, Paris, and Achilles,
> Eleyne, Cleopatre, and Troylus,
> Silla, and ek the moder of Romulus:
> Alle these were peynted on that other syde,
> And al here love, and in what plyt they dyde. (288-294)

Again I emphasize that no direct associations are made with
Fortuna, but Venus' garden, with its personifications of courtly
love abstractions, is contrasted with the realm of Natura. Though
the park is beautiful, it is at one remove from actuality, more
suggestive of the tableau than of life. And running throughout –

from landscape and natural world to legends on the wall – are suggestions of a progression from life to death as the mortal enters deeper and deeper into the kingdom of the goddess of love.

As already suggested in the earlier description, Natura's garden contains none of the tableau effect of Venus' garden. From the moment the Dreamer-Narrator sees the queen beautiful "as of lyght the somer sonne shene / Passeth the sterre" (299-300) seated on her hill of flowers, the legend on the other gate echoes implicitly:

> Thorgh me men gon into that blysful place
> Of hertes hele and dedly woundes cure;
> Thorgh me men gon unto the welle of grace,
> There grene and lusty May shal evere endure.   (127-130)

The validity of the legend is borne out in the description of Natura, who appears, the Dreamer-Narrator says, "right as Aleyn, in the Pleynt of Kynde, / Devyseth Nature of aray and face" (316-317). In Alain, Natura's crown, her robe, her shoes, all parts of her raiment are wondrously composed of living representations of all animal creation.[36] To Alain and – by Chaucer's own association – to Chaucer, Natura is not a deity of tangible proportions. Just as the articles of her clothing contain all life and continually enact the organic principle of existance, so she herself is all life. She partakes of the macrocosm and the microcosm. The garden and the birds in Chaucer's poem, like the objects on her clothing, are separate from her and yet they are part of her. She is in the garden and yet she is the garden. One detail which points up the organic relationship between Natura and her realm lies in the number of times (a total of fifteen, counting the two references upon the Narrator's first entrance into the park[37]) Chaucer uses the words "kind" and "nature" in describing her garden. The Narrator notices trees "Ech in his kynde" (174), "Squyrels, and bestes smale of gentil kynde" (196), "othere egles of a lowere kynde" (332), "of foules

---

[36]   De Planctu: PL, CCX: 282. 18ff through 287. 15.
[37]   Lines 174, 196, 303, 311, 316, 332, 358, 360, 365, 401, 434, 450, 457, 601, 615. (List includes references to "unkind".)

every kynde" (365). Even though he means the words in their general sense, the associations with the goddess are reinforced at every repetition. Thus through the use of puns upon the name of Natura, goddess of kind, he makes the suggestion that, even as in Alain's *De Planctu*, she and her realm are the same.

In this garden, where Natura, "the vicaire of the almyghty Lord" (379) is the ruling power, the scene, in contrast with the garden of Venus, is one of joyous and noisy activity. The only complication of the Valentine Day mating comes when the element of courtly love enters in the dispute over the formel eagle. Natura herself, with her ultimate purpose of generation of the species, is eager to have the birds mate and insists only that the requisites of order and degree be observed in choice. Significantly, Natura gives the choice to the tercel, not the formel. It is the three male eagles who automatically hand the power of choice to the lady eagle and turn the mating session into a courtly debate. They even speak in terms which directly recall the arrows of Cupid, the lorn lovers, and the legend on the gate of the garden of Venus (421-427, 452-453, 471-473). Natura allows the suitors to carry through the courtly theme, listens to the birds' chaotic attempts to judge, and finally – allowing free will, as love must – gives the choice to the formel on her wrist. She even offers advice to the lady eagle, but not in her person as Natura. " 'If I were Resoun . . .' " (632), she counsels, entering into the courtly game.[38] But Natura is not Resoun,[39] and the formel eagle is Natura's creature: " 'My rightful lady, goddesse of Nature! / Soth is that I am evere under your yerde, . . . / And mot be youres whil my lyf may dure' " (639-640, 642). Thus she spurns the choice which involves following the court-of-love tradition; instead, she asks for a year's respite " 'and after that to

---

[38] In the *Roman* (4221ff) part of the courtly lover's ritual involves listening at length to the counsel of Reason. At the end of the poem, however, amid Jean de Meun's sexual imagery when the lover wins the Rose and thanks those who have helped him, he remarks, "Mais de Raison ne me souvint, / Qui tant en mei gasta de peine" (21760-21761).

[39] Frank, p. 538, uses this detail effectively to indicate that the comedy of the poem rises from the "iron whim" of love in action. Huppé and Robertson (p. 140) link Natura, as God's vicar, with Reason and Grace.

have my choys al fre / ... I wol nat serve Venus ne Cupide, / Forsothe as yit, by no manere weye' " (649, 652-653). She implicitly links Venus and Cupid with the bondage of the unfree choice of courtly conventions and totally rejects this hindrance. Her decision does not by implication link Natura and chastity; rather, it emphasizes the freedom of Natura's love from all external ritual and trappings. The small birds, who represent the rule to the formel's exception, are constantly outspoken in their disapproval of the courtly proceedings, and the poem ends with the birds' hymn of joy after they have straightway chosen mates upon Natura's command. Part of the meaning of the poem, therefore, springs from the contrast between the process of love according to Natura and according to the courtly tradition. In the *Parliament* the two kinds of love do not preclude each other. There are hints of Natura on the threshold of Venus' realm; Natura is tolerant toward the courtly debate, and the failure of love according to courtly tradition in her domain does not have the overtones of frustration which are present in Venus' temple. But the difference between the kinds of love emerges. The suitor-eagles are discomfited and the formel unmated because of courtly trappings; the humbler fowl, who do not complicate their love, are more joyous than the lovers in the temple of Venus. I do not suggest that Chaucer here advocates rejecting Venus for Natura. Since the Dreamer-Narrator feels that the vision of the mating birds resolves nothing, part of Chaucer's point may be the near-impossibility of a completely "natural" love for complicated humanity.

In this introductory chapter I have attempted two general tasks. First, I have discussed the literary sources and the popular traditions for Chaucer's use of Natura and Fortuna as clashing destinal agents. Second, I have examined Chaucer's miscellaneous uses of Fortuna and Natura. When the influence of one deity is significant in a narrative, the influence of the other shadows the background except in the religious tales, where the goddesses appear singly as agents of God. In the "Monk's Tale", the *Troilus* and the *Parliament* the veiled conflict points up the inherent philosophical themes of the poems; in all three, though the

Christian background is assumed, the goddesses betray pagan shadows of absoluteness. The following chapters will examine the three narratives in which – in addition to the *Book of the Duchess* – Chaucer uses the Natura-Fortuna opposition, fully developed, for fundamental dramatic and thematic purposes.

II. THE "PHYSICIAN'S TALE"

The purpose of this chapter is to analyze one dimension of literary technique in the "Physician's Tale"; the relationship of this and the other tales to the framework of the Canterbury pilgrimage will not be considered. Scholarly criticism dealing with the "Physician's Tale" itself concentrates upon the character of Virginia. Scholars analyze her maidenly virtues, associating her with Mary or the "consecrated virgin" tradition of the Church Fathers; [1] and they point out that the tale is her personal and pathetic tragedy.[2] Patch's comment upon her character is exaggerated but typical: "The virtuous ladies, I am afraid, are conventional or vague in these stories on the way to Canterbury. The portrait of Virginia in the 'Physician's Tale' begins with the favors bestowed by Dame Nature; as in the case of Emelye her color vies with that of the rose and the lily, or something of the sort ... In conduct she might have been the Parson, in speech the Clerk, in morality and abstinence a veritable Sir Thopas." [3] Most critics mention that Natura is the agent of Virginia's creation, but no one assigns the goddess a functional role in the tale. Robinson, commenting about the lines on Natura, states that medieval authors often represent the goddess as giving special

[1] Frederick Tupper, "Chaucer's Bed's Head", *MLN*, XXX (1951), 5-7; Karl Young, "The Maidenly Virtues of Chaucer's Virginia", *Speculum*, XVI (1941), 340-349.
[2] Germaine Dempster, *Dramatic Irony in Chaucer* (Stanford, 1932), p. 92n.; R. D. French, *A Chaucer Handbook*, 2nd ed. (New York, 1947), p. 267; R. M. Lumiansky, *Of Sondry Folk* (Austin, 1955), p. 197; R. K. Root, *The Poetry of Chaucer* (New York, 1906), p. 222.
[3] H. R. Patch, *On Rereading Chaucer* (Cambridge, Mass., 1939), p. 180.

attention to the creation of a beautiful woman.[4] But if Chaucer simply wanted to show Natura's interest in beauty, a single couplet would do as well: "But she was yit the fayreste creature / That evere was yformed by Nature" (*LGW*, 974-975). Tupper asserts that Chaucer uses the section on Natura and on Virginia's qualities of perfection to develop his treatment of the vice of Lechery through its antitype Chastity.[5] But the judge in Gower's version of the Appius and Virginia story emerges as the epitome of lechery without any mention of Natura.[6] The tale is too short for Chaucer to intend his lengthy description of Natura as digression or as reinforcement of a theme which does not need such obvious support. It seems to me that the role of Natura is functional, and, indeed, fundamental to the meaning of the story. Chaucer's description of her is not preliminary to the tale; it is the beginning of the tale. And the conflict which the tale presents is as much celestial as it is terrestrial. Thus the narrative from the beginning assumes overtones of allegory, though finally it is not, on this level, allegorical. In Chaucer's version of the Appius and Virginia story, Natura's sovereignty is put to the test by earthly forces of evil resembling Fortuna. Virginius, Virginia, and Appius — none of whom Chaucer individualizes as characters — appear stylized for a reason: they are actors who give the conflict its human representation. Natura fully as much as Virginia is the protagonist of the "Physician's Tale".

The tone of Chaucer's version is markedly different from that of his sources and from that of Gower's contemporary narrative. Livy, Chaucer's acknowledged source, is concerned with moral historiography, and his sprawling chronicle of the episode is frankly nationalistic: Appius' lust-motivated attempt to use Roman law to achieve possession of Virginia sets off a chain of events that culminates in the downfall of the corrupt decemvir

---

[4] Line references to the "Physician's Tale" are to Fragment VI. For a discussion of Natura and beautiful women, see also E. C. Knowlton, "Nature in Old French", *MP*, XX (1923), 310ff.

[5] Tupper, p. 5.

[6] *Confessio Amantis*, VII. 5131-5306 — in G. C. Macaulay (ed.), *The Complete Works of John Gower*, Vol. III (Oxford, 1901).

government in 449 B. C. Livy's purpose is to demonstrate that
officials who "nimis luxuriaverunt" [7] must fall. Jean de Meun,
Chaucer's immediate source, tells the incident concerning Appius
and Virginia as part of a diatribe against the wickedness and
injustice of court judges. "Briement juige font trop d'outrages", [8]
runs his moral tag. Gower, whose version was published later
thans Chaucer's, [9] didactically announces that he intends the story
as an *exemplum* to prove that " . . . rihtwisnesse and lecherie /
Accorden noght in compaignie / With him that hath the lawe
on honde." In all the versions, including Chaucer's, the outline
of the narrative is the same. Chaucer's tale overtly resembles the
others in its didacticism against wickedness: "Heere may men
seen how synne hath his merite . . . . / Therfore I rede yow this
conseil take: / Forsaketh synne, er synne yow forsake" (277;
285-286), moralizes the narrator at the end. But the moral tag
does not square with Chaucer's focus in his tale. The changes
which Chaucer makes from Jean de Meun's narrative occur on
a level beyond the literal. His innovations appear as two major
additions which deepen the tone and theme: first, the section
dealing with Natura and Virginia's qualities of perfection (19-
120); and, second, the scene describing Virginius' final meeting
with his daughter just before he kills her (207-253).

The religious tone of the tale is obvious. Virginia's virtues, as
mentioned earlier, are those of church tradition; the wicked judge
is moved to evil by the "feend". But the action is not motivated
in conventionally Christian terms. The supernatural figure who
appears is Natura who, though agent of God, acts from primal
creative depths ("sovereyn diligence" – 9). The Host's comment
on the tale sets it more readily in popular than in patristic tradition:

---

[7]   Livy, *Ab Urbe Condita*, Loeb Classical Library (New York, 1922),
p. 108.
[8]   Line 5659. The entire episode in the *Roman*: 5589-5794.
[9]   W. F. Bryan and Germaine Dempster, *Sources and Analogues of
Chaucer's "Canterbury Tales"* (New York, 1958), p. 398; J. S. P. Tatlock,
The Development and Chronology of Chaucer's Works (London, 1907),
pp. 150-156; Gower, *Confessio Amantis*, VII. 5124-5126.

"Wherfore I seye al day that men may see
That yiftes of Fortune and of Nature
Been cause of deeth to many a creature.
Hire beautee was hire deth, I dar wel sayn.
Allas, so pitously as she was slayn!
Of bothe yiftes that I speke of now
Men han ful ofte moore for harm than prow." (294-300)

His judgment of the roles of the goddesses, as one might expect, is askew. Fortuna's machinations, not Natura's gifts, are Virginia's "cause of deeth". But his linking of the goddesses identifies the forces which work behind the surface of the narrative. Chaucer in veiled fashion indicates the workings of Fortuna in the tale. He mentions Envy, "that sory is of oother mennes wele, / And glad is of his sorwe and his unheele" (115-116). And Envy, says the Parson, is "a synne agayns kynde" (X. 491). Chaucer creates Appius with broad resemblances to Fortuna. Appius is a governor, wielding absolute worldly power; he is a judge, ruling without regard for right or justice. The epithet which Chaucer most often uses for him is "false",[10] a stock epithet for Fortuna. Though the tale remains essentially Christian, Chaucer broadens the dramatic scope by stepping outside Christian terminology for his dramatic focus.

Basically, in this tale Chaucer poses a philosophical dilemma for the goddess Natura. In the first lines he establishes her sovereignty over living things. Then he questions this sovereignty dramatically through the story of Appius and Virginia in which lechery and death, both enemies of Natura, threaten the goddess's human agents with a situation in which they have no alternative but to choose between two evils. The crucial questions are, first, which they will choose (lechery or death); and, second, whether they can escape the dilemma while remaining completely true to the principles of Natura.

Natura's speech at the beginning of the poem precipitates the

---

[10] "This false juge, that highte Apius ..." (154); "This false juge gooth now faste aboute ..." (158); "This false juge, as telleth us the storie ..." (161); "'Thus hath he falsly jugged the to-day'" (228). Appius' minion Claudius is "this fals cherl" (164). The people rise up against Appius because "... knowen was the false iniquitee" (262).

conflict. The maiden Virginia is a creation of such perfection
that Natura is completely delighted and charmed with her, and
the goddess cannot keep silent about her own handiwork:

> For Nature hath with sovereyn diligence
> Yformed hire in so greet excellence,
> As though she wolde seyn, "Lo! I, Nature,
> Thus kan I forme and peynte a creature,
> Whan that me list; who kan me countrefete?
> Pigmalion noght, though he ay forge and bete,
> Or grave, or peynte; for I dar wel seyn,
> Apelles, Zanzis, sholde werche in veyn
> Outher to grave, or peynte, or forge, or bete,
> If they presumed me to countrefete.
> For He that is the formere principal
> Hath maked me his vicaire general,
> To forme and peynten erthely creaturis
> Right as me list, and ech thyng in my cure is
> Under the moone, that may wane and waxe;
> And for my werk right no thyng wol I axe;
> My lord and I been ful of oon accord.
> I made hire to the worshipe of my lord;
> So do I alle myne othere creatures,
> What colour that they han, or what figures."   (9-28)

In this speech Natura praises the maiden Virginia as the paragon
of her creative passion. Further, she defines her own position in
the universe in no uncertain terms: she speaks in a tone of absolute authority, emphasizing first her own power and next her
close relationship with all-powerful God. She and she alone can
create beauty in living things. She works effortlessly, but her
productions are matchless. The most skillful artists which all the
ages of man have produced are totally incapable of duplicating
one of her creations, and they are quite presumptuous even to
try to duplicate her work. She emphasizes her power as unique:
"Thus kan I forme . . . ; who kan me countrefete? Pigmalion . . .
Apelles, Zanzis, sholde werche in veyn . . . If they presumed me
to countrefete." Next, she gives her power even greater implications by pointing out her direct link with God the Creator. God
has named her His "vicaire general": He charges her to carry
out the sacred work of creation and gives her dominion over all

living creatures. Further, He gives her a free hand in her duties to perform them "whan that me list" and "right as me list". Natura acknowledges readily that her power proceeds from the higher power of heaven, and, accordingly, she shapes her every creation as an act of worship to God. But she is completely confident in her own ability as God's excutive. She seeks help or advice from no other agency. She is responsible only to God, and she is so perfect an agent that her will accords in every detail with His divine will.

As the introduction discussed, Chaucer is in accord with tradition in framing Natura's authority thus. His deepening of tradition lies first, as mentioned above, in his emphasis on the profundity of Natura's creative authority,[11] and second, in the strength and exclusiveness of the bond between Natura, man, and God. In the *Roman*, for example, Jean de Meun emphasizes more strongly man's obligation to Natura than he does Natura's to man or to God. In the *Anticlaudianus*, Natura does not approach God with her request that He allow her to create the human race anew; she sends Prudence, assisted by the seven Liberal Arts, as emissary.[12] In *De Planctu*, Genius and Hymen

---

[11] The impulse comes from *De Consolatione*, where Nature and God are sometimes loosely equated, and from the *Roman*:

"It liketh me to schewe by subtil song, with slakke and delytable sown of strenges, how that Nature, myghty, enclyneth and flytteth the governementz of thynges, and by whiche lawes sche, purveiable, kepith the grete world; and how sche, byndynge, restreyneth alle thynges by a boond that may nat be unbownde" (III. meter 2. 1-7).

> Mais ci ne peüst il riens faire,
> Zeusis, tant seüst bien pourtraire,
> Ne coulourer sa pourtraiture,
> Tant est de grant beauté Nature.
> Zeusis! non pas trestuit li maistre
> Que Nature fist onques naistre;
> Car, or seit que bien entendissent
> Sa beauté toute, e tuit vousissent
> A tel pourtraiture muser,
> Ainz pourraient leur mains user
> Que si trés grant beauté pourtraire.
> Nus fors Deus ne le pourrait faire. (16199-16210)

[12] II. 310-513.

play prominent roles as Natura's assistants.[13] In Machaut's *Prologue* Natura relates to man through her children, Scens, Retorique, and Musique.[14] Though such accompanying personifications are usual in other authors, Chaucer simplifies the destinal hierarchy by ignoring these lesser agents who appear and by giving Natura sole authority as God's executor. His single focus upon her magnifies her power and gives her statement its authoritative tone.

Natura's speech is not proud or boastful; it is matter-of-fact. Perhaps the goddess preens a bit in delight over her creation of Virginia: "Lo, I, Nature", she begins with regal satisfaction. At any rate, Natura, the universal creative force, is challenged by the primal force of destruction (by implication, Fortuna) so that Natura must prove her lordship over her own creations. The fickle goddess strikes at her through the onslaught on Virginia, who is the mortal exemplification of Natura's lordly speech. Virginius and Virginia, the two characters upon whom the disaster falls, are the instruments through whom Natura is vindicated, although in the process they become more than instruments. Virginia is obviously Natura's paragon. In fact, her maidenly virtues seem to belong as much to the tradition of Natura and her handmaidens as to the tradition of the Church Fathers: Chaucer's list of her beauties and virtues broadly parallels the perfect qualities of Natura and her votaresses in *De Planctu Naturae*.[15] Natura, like Virginia, is lily-white and rosered with golden tresses. She herself is chaste, and Chastity is the first of her votaresses to come to the council. Temperance (Virginia's "attemperaunce" and "abstinence") and Humility (Virginia's "humylitee" and "pacience") follow Chastity to Natura's council. Natura and her handmaidens constantly show "mesure eek of beryng and array" (45). Natura possesses powers of eloquence like Virginia's "facound eek ful wommanly and pleyn"

[13]   *PL*, CCX. 315-320.
[14]   *Prologue*, I, Part I. 1-27, Part II. 1-27 (lyric dialogue between Nature and the poet).
[15]   Natura's physical appearance: *PL*, CCX. 282. 21-36. Natura's chastity: 283.57. Votaresses Chastity – 313.1-48 – Temperance – 313.49-314.3 – Humility – 314.51-315.5. Natura's warning against Bacchus: 311.61-72.

(50). The goddess does not use "countrefeted termes" (51) but she speaks her wisdom plainly, and her arguments heal Alain's sick soul. Natura, throughout *De Planctu Naturae*, is "in bisynesse" (56) as she cares for her world of natural creatures. Finally, for Natura, as for Virginia, "Bacus hadde of hir mouth right no maistrie" (58); and she warns Alain to beware of the draughts and madness of Bacchus.

In my opinion, critics have not sufficiently emphasized the importance of Virginius in the tale. He rather than Virginia is Natura's positive and assertive force for good: he appears before the judge, who stops him from proving that Claudius is a liar (191-198); he makes the decision that Virginia must die (223-226); he boldly faces the judge afterward in court (255-257); and he asks the people to commute Claudius' sentence from death to exile (272-273). Thus, Virginius represents active good and Virginia is passive acceptance of that good. Their functions are complementary, but Virginius' role is the harder of the two: Virginia, Natura's paragon, must die; he, her father, must kill. The Roman custom of calling a daughter by the feminine form of her father's *gens* name here serves a definite function. The nearly identical names show the inseparable association of father and daughter working to overcome evil.

Chaucer organizes the human conflict in the tale around the two "sentences" which determine Virginia's fate – Appius' verdict and Virginius' counter-verdict. In the events which lead up to the judgment of Appius, Chaucer follows the narrative details of his sources. The judge sees Virginia, and

> Anon his herte chaunged and his mood,
> So was he caught with beautee of this mayde,
> And to hymself ful pryvely he sayde,
> "This mayde shal be myn, for any man!"   (126-129)

Ironically, the sight of her virtuous perfection changes his heart and mood to evil, not to good: "Anon the feend into his herte ran, / And taughte hym sodeynly that he by slyghte / The mayden to his purpos wynne myghte" (130-132). With the help of his minion Claudius he carries out his scheme, making a show of impartiality. He hands down his judgment, triumphantly condemning Natura's paragon to his own lustful desires, and thus destructive Fortuna's challenge to life-giving Natura is accomplished.

In his second major addition to the tale – the encounter between Virginius and Virginia after Appius gives his verdict – Chaucer presents as he faces her dilemma:

> And whan this worthy knyght Virginius,
> Thurgh sentence of this justice Apius,
> Moste by force his deere doghter yiven
> Unto the juge, in lecherie to lyven,
> He gooth hym hoom, and sette him in his halle,
> And leet anon his deere doghter calle,
> And with a face deed as asshen colde
> Upon hir humble face he gan biholde,
> With fadres pitee stikynge thurgh his herte,
> Al wolde he from his purpos nat converte.   (203-212)

Natura hates lust. The passionate eloquence of Alain's *De Planctu* represents the classic statement of the goddess Natura's loathing for unnatural appetites. Natura cannot remain sovereign and allow Virginia, the personification of her creative love, to become the slave of the lecherous judge. Equally strongly, however, Natura hates death, the final negation of her creative power. In the *Roman*, one of Natura's major tasks is to out-do death, to perpetuate the species and help it flourish in the face of death's opposition.[16] Violent or premature death is especially abhorrent to the goddess of kind. Virginius sees that submission to Appius' verdict is out of the question. Even in the face of Natura's hatred of death, he sees and accepts the alternative to submission:

[16] For example:

C'est fenis la comune fourme
Que Nature es pieces refourme,
Qui dou tout perdue serait,
Que l'autre vivre ne lairait.
Cete maniere neïs ont
Trestoutes les choses qui sont
Desouz le cercle de la lune
Que, s'il en peut demourer l'une,
S'espiece tant en li vivra
Que ja Mort ne l'aconsivra.

Mais Nature douce e piteuse,
Quant el veit que Mort l'envieuse,
Entre li e Corrupcion,
Vienent metre a destruccion
Quanqu'eus treuvent dedenz sa forge,
Toujourz martele, toujourz forge,
Toujourz ses pieces renouvele
Par generacion nouvele.
(15995-16012)

" 'Doghter', quod he, 'Virginia, by thy name, / Ther been two weyes, outher deeth or shame, / That thou most suffre' " (213-215). Since the mandates of Natura leave him trapped, he makes the only decision possible by exerting the agony of human will to transcend Natura and act in accord with a higher principle of love than that which demands life at all costs. Chaucer, as we see here, in some contexts regards Natura as a limited figure. She represents love, but not the highest love which the human spirit can attain. As Chaucer translates and glosses the same issue in the *Boece*: "For certes in the beestis [animalibus] the love of hire lyvynges ne of hire beynges ne cometh not of the wilnynges of the soule, but of the bygynnynges of nature. For certes, thurw constreynynge causes, wil desireth and embraceth ful ofte tyme the deeth that nature dredeth. (*That is to seyn as thus: that a man may be constreyned so, by some cause, that his wille desireth and taketh the deeth which that nature hateth and dredeth ful sore*)" (III. prose 11. 159-168).

Virginius laments that Virginia must die, but he laments even more that she must die by his hand. His role is agonizing (" 'allas, that I was bore!' " – 215), and he expresses Natura's anguish at seeing the wasteful destruction of the beloved creation which the goddess has shaped through his agency: " . . . nevere thou deservedest wherfore / To dyen with a swerd or with a knyf" (216-217). Virginia is his child. She is so much a part of his existence through Natura's bond of blood kinship that he virtually shares in her experience of death:

> O deere doghter, endere of my lyf,
> Which I have fostred up with swich plesaunce
> That thou were nevere out of my remembraunce!
> O doghter, which that art my laste wo,
> And in my lyf my laste joye also . . . . (218-222)

Thus through his tortured "wilnynges of soule" he hands down a "sentence" upon the goddess' unique creation:

> O gemme of chastitee, in pacience
> Take thou thy deeth, for this is my sentence.
> For love, and nat for hate, thou most be deed;
> My pitous hand moot smyten of thyn heed. (223-226)

Virginia at first cannot accept the judgment; her station as a child of Natura forbids her. She reflects Natura's basic ambivalence toward the necessity of death, the goddess' reluctance to accept untimely death even as an escape from the evil of lechery:

> "O mercy, deere fader!" quod this mayde,
> And with that word she both hir armes layde
> Aboute his nekke, as she was wont to do.
> The teeris bruste out of his eyen two,
> And seyde, "Goode fader, shal I dye?
> Is ther no grace, is ther no remedye?"   (231-236)

But Virginius cannot allow either himself or his daughter to flinch. To save Virginia he must act unstintingly and unreservedly through love. He cannot follow the principles of love and hand over his daughter to Appius "in lecherie to lyven"; but he can slay her in love and save her from the hell of Appius' evil, if she accepts Virginius' sentence of her own volition. Virginia, through the strength that is hers in the bond of human kinship,[17] rises above the limits of Natura and accepts her father's decision. She laments the necessity of her death, but she does not, as does "Jepte's doghter", ask "that I may go up and down upon the mountains, and bewail my virginity, I and my fellows" (Judges 11 : 37). Instead, she swoons. Mystically. when she recovers, she is not reconciled but exultant: " 'Blissed be God, that I shall dye a mayde! / Yif me my deeth, er that I have a shame; / Dooth with your child youre wyl, a Goddes name!' " (248-250). Thus, Virginius cuts off her head "with ful sorweful herte and wil" (254). But Virginius' slaying and Virginia's death do not proceed from panic and desperation; they represent an act of triumph. In Livy and Gower, the father neatly stabs the daughter, but in Chaucer's version the gore of Virginia's severed head points up the irony that Natura's children should reach moral and spiritual victory in a welter of blood. Virginius, to the end the assertive force for good, carries the triumph to its conclusion by effecting the downfall of the false judge, representative of Fortuna, when he faces Appius in court.

[17] Note the frequent repetition of the words "doghter" (237, 240), "child" (250), and "fader" (231, 235, 238, 243, 247) from lines 231-250.

The destructive forces of Fortuna implied in the tale are, of course, roundly defeated. As far as possible, Natura in the "Physician's Tale" is faithful to her cardinal principle of love. Chaucer's point, however, is that, just as Fortuna's destructive tyranny is never a worthy basis for human action, even so Natura's love is not always sufficient for human need. Because both father and daughter agree in love that Virginia must die, she meets her death in victory, not in defeat; and in approaching a love like that of God himself, so powerful that it can create good from evil, both father and daughter assume a spiritual transcendence beyond the laws of Natura. Thus, though the tale moves on dramatic levels more complex than those of allegory, the Fortuna-Natura overtones lend depth to the Christian theme.

III. THE "CLERK'S TALE"

The "Physician's Tale", with Natura appearing as a character, approaches allegory; the "Clerk's Tale", too casts shadows of allegory, though not so heavily as the "Physician's Tale". In the story of patient Griselda the dramatic focus from the beginning lies upon the human rather than upon the supernatural agents. Recent scholars who have examined the "Clerk's Tale" apart from the liveliness of its dramatic context consider it primarily as Chaucer's skillful verse translation of the prose version by Petrarch or his French translator,[1] as his handling of an ancient folk-motif,[2] or as pure Christian allegory.[3] There are no all-out defenders of the tale, but two critics, James Sledd and E. T. Donaldson,[4] find in it original and artistic handling of theme and characterization. I am disposed to credit Chaucer with originality and artistry in his use of Fortuna and Natura as literary symbols in the "Clerk's Tale" because, with several explicit references to

---

[1] J. Burke Severs, "The Literary Relationships of Chaucer's *Clerkes Tale*", *Yale Studies in English*, XCVI (New York, 1942), 215-248. He notes Chaucer's "unity of conception and spirit" (p. 248) but emphasizes the close relationship of the poem to its sources.

[2] W. A. Cate, "The Problem of the Origin of the Griselda Story", *SP*, XXIX (1932), 389-405; D. D. Griffith, *The Origin of the Griselda Story* (Seattle, 1931); Severs, pp. 3-41. James Sledd, "The *Clerk's Tale*: The Monsters and the Critics", *MP*, LI (1953), 73-82, presents a critical summary of scholarship on this interpretation.

[3] Marchette Chute, *Geoffrey Chaucer of England* (New York, 1946), p. 281; Kemp Malone, *Chapters on Chaucer* (Baltimore, 1951), p. 223.

[4] Sledd, pp. 77-79; E. T. Donaldson, *Chaucer's Poetry* (New York, 1958), pp. 917-920.

these deities as a basis,[5] he reflects their traits in the two major characters and thus shapes on the human level a conflict and a triumph which run as a corollary to Petrarch's moral tag and which give the poem an added dimension. Walter is so closely identified with Fortuna and Griselda with Natura that each character posseses the characteristics of the governing semi-deity, with a deeper victory for Griselda in that, just as Virginia, she transcends even the endurance of the goddess of Kind. Walter is not Fortuna and Griselda is not Natura, but an association of the principal characters with the agents of Providence does seem to me to underlie the tale for the purpose of focusing the human conflict in the poem.

In order to set Fortuna and Natura as background deities, Chaucer makes several significant changes from his acknowledged source, Petrarch's "De Insigni Obedientia et Fide Uxoris", and from his second source, the anonymous French translation of Petrarch's epistle. First, he plays up the importance of Natura in the passages dealing with Griselda. He characterizes her as consistently "kynde", a term which can here be interpreted in its root meaning of "natural", and his mention of the goddess, lacking in the sources, comes at the height of his heroine's misfortunes. More significantly, in the first two parts, Chaucer deemphasizes the influence of Fortuna in Griselda's career. In Petrarch there are two references to Griselda's doing something *fortune*,[6] "paraventure" or "by chance", which Chaucer deletes from his own narrative. In Chaucer's version Fortuna, chance, *aventure* and *cas* play no part in Griselda's existence until after she has come under Walter's control. Conversely, Chaucer emphasizes the importance of Fortuna's role in Walter's affairs.

---

[5] Chaucer mentions Natura once (line 902) and Fortuna four times (69, 756, 812, and 898). Line references to the "Clerk's Tale" are to Fragment IV.

[6] References to the Latin and French texts are to W. F. Bryan and Germaine Dempster, *Sources and Analogues of Chaucer's "Canterbury Tales"* (New York, 1958), pp. 296-331. Petrarch says, "vicissimque domum rediens, oluscula et dapes fortune congruas preparabat" (p. 302); "Hinc ne quid reliquiarum fortune veteris novam inferret in domum, nudari eam iussit, et a calce ad verticem novis vestibus indui" (p. 306). The references to *fortune* are not in the French translation.

Critics commonly observe that Chaucer heightens Walter's cruelty, making him appear unnecessarily severe, harsher than he is in either Petrarch or the French redactor. It seems to me that this heightening of his irrational cruelty serves to increase the resemblance of his behavior to that of the goddess Fortuna. Chaucer also directly associates Walter with Fortuna in the first stanzas of the poem through a significant detail of exposition lacking in the sources.[7] Later, in Griselda's stanzas of gentle lament, which are Chaucer's independent addition, Chaucer by implication denies any connection between Natura and Walter: Griselda regrets that she has misjudged him and thought him "kynde".

Chaucer effects his most significant single departure from his sources by immediately linking Walter with Fortuna as his controlling deity:

> A markys whilom lord was of that lond,
> As were his worthy eldres hym bifore;
> And obeisant, ay redy to his hond,
> Were alle his liges, bothe lasse and moore.
> Thus in delit he lyveth, and hath doon yoore,
> Biloved and drad, thurgh favour of Fortune,
> Bothe of his lordes and of his commune.   (64-70)

Walter is Fortuna's darling. He is noble, dashing, and attractive, and he has many splendid qualities of character. But his virtues are of a worldly sort – courtly honor and courtesy and ability to govern his country adequately – and they are counterbalanced by the "somme thynges" in which he is "to blame" – his lack of concern with the serious side of life and his refusal to marry. Like Fortuna herself, Walter has no eye for past or future:

[7] Petrarch: "unus primusque omnium et maximus fuisse traditur Valterius quidam, ad quem familie ac terrarum omnium regimen pertineret; et hic quidem forma virens atque etate, nec minus moribus quam sanguine nobilis, et ad summam omni ex parte vir insignis" (p. 296 and 298).

French: "Le premier et le plus grant on treuve avoir esté un marquis appelez en son propre nom Wautier, auquel principaument appartenoit le gouvernement et dominacion d'icelle terre. Bel et jeune seigneur estoit, moult noble de lignaige et plus assez en bonnes meurs, et en somme noble en toutes manieres" (p. 297 and 299).

Chaucer's lines (64-70) are quoted in the body of my text.

> . . . he considered noght
> In tyme comynge what myghte hym bityde,
> But on his lust present was al his thoght,
> As for to hauke and hunte on every syde. (78-80)

Though he is "discreet ynogh his contree for to gye" (75), he
leaves the state to its own devices so that he may follow his own
delightful but transitory pleasures. He lives only for immediate
delight, and about himself and his people he is quite happily
improvident.

With the immediate reference to Fortuna in the two stanzas
of introduction to the young marquis, Walter's character is established, and the role he plays as the narrative unfolds makes
him seen almost a representation of the fickle goddess in human
lineaments. Again, Walter is not merely an allegorical shadow;
the Narrator's bewildered comments on Walter's action focus the
reader's speculation upon the young lord's human roots. The
similarities between Walter and Fortuna, however, are pervasive
and vital in the tale. Like Fortuna, he is tyrannical, demanding
absolute mastery over whatever he touches. His subjects bow and
kneel before him and thank him humbly for deigning to do his
duty to the state and marry (186-188). Griselda serves him, as
he makes her promise to do (351-357), in complete obedience.
Throughout the tale his underlings – notably the court ladies and
the sergeant (374, 519-525, 582-589) – hasten to carry out his
will while he sits back and gives orders.

For Walter, as for Fortuna, whim becomes reality in a flash:
he, like her, is characterized by impulsive decisions and actions
which result in disaster for those people under his control. Walter's desire to test his wife by snatching away her baby daughter
springs from an irrational whim:

> This markys in his herte longeth so
> To tempte his wyf, hir sadnesse for to knowe,
> That he ne myghte out of his herte throwe
> This merveillous desir his wyf t'assaye. (451-454)

Similarly, after the next child comes, " . . . on a day / This markys
caughte yet another lest / To tempte his wyf yet ofter, if he may"
(618-620). Walter, like Fortuna, does nothing half-way. Just as

Fortuna turns her wheel to plummet her subjects from prosperity to ruin, weal to woe, so Walter does not cease to plague Griselda with his testing until he has stripped from her all appurtenances of honor and plunged her into a state of "wo and peyne". Chaucer emphasizes repeatedly throughout the testing episodes that Walter's actions are puzzling, capricious, and irrational. "What neded it / Hire for to tempte, and alway moore and moore, / Though som men preise it for a subtil wit?" (457-459) he wonders when the idea first strikes Walter. He conjectures that Walter may be acting cruelly "for ernest" or "for game"; ultimately he cannot explain Walter's decision to test Griselda as logical or understandable.

Walter, like Fortuna, is completely unpredictable. Although Chaucer in some measure prepares the reader for the twists of the narrative, Walter's actions burst with shock force upon the other characters in the tale. From beginning to end, the other characters remain in uncertainty and dread because no one but Walter himself knows what he is about. When he agrees to marry, he hints oddly to his subjects that his choice of a wife may not be at all conventional, and they are alarmed lest he not marry at all. When the day of the wedding arrives, the people are anxious and resentful because they have no notion of what Walter proposes to do: " 'Wol nat oure lord yet leve his vanytee? / Wol he nat wedde? allas; allas, the while! / Why wole he thus hymself and us bigile?' " (250-252). When Walter announces that he intends to marry Griselda, Janicula is thunderstruck: "This sodeyn cas this man astonyed so / That reed he wax; abayst and al quakynge / He stood" (316-318). When Walter suddenly appears at the ox-stall, Griselda is almost overcome, and she is stunned by his proposal, to which she agrees, "quakynge for drede" (358). Griselda retains her equanimity at every phase of the testing, but her presence of mind does not negate the abruptness with which Walter announces his intention on each occasion. Because of his unpredictable actions the people turn against him. Walter's final announcement – that all the torture has been a trick, that the children are alive, and that he loves her and wants her for his wife once more – comes as such an unexpected revelation to Griselda that she faints. Throughout the tale, then, Chaucer effects such a close association between Walter and Fortuna that Walter's every major trait of character parallels a trait characteristic of the fickle goddess. He represents one extreme human alternative. In a world which, according to his actions, he regards as governed by chance, he attempts a symbiosis between himself and the universe by reinforcing the fickle tutelage of Fortuna with his own whimsical actions. Since he acknowledges no order, he acts with none.

Griselda, on the other hand, represents the other extreme – creative submission rather than wilful dominance. Up to a point, her actions proceed from her affinity with the goddess Natura; in many ways she is Natura's child. She is one of the "povre folk of that village", daughter of the "povrest of hem all", but she is poor only in the transitory regalia of worldly prosperity. Poverty, because it has made her live close to the world of Natura, has given her unique riches of beauty and character:

> But for to speke of vertuous beautee,
> Thanne was she oon the faireste under sonne;
> For povreliche yfostred up was she,
> No likerous lust was thurgh hire herte yronne.   (211-214)

Her life is neither burdensome nor unhappy but productive, uncomplicated, and blessed with the grace of God. The little "throop" stands on a "site delitable" and the earth yields "habundance". Griselda lives close to the land: she keeps a few sheep in the pasture; she gathers from Natura's plenty a few simple "wortes or othere herbes tymes ofte, / The whiche she shredde and seeth for hir lyvynge" (226-227); she drinks "wel ofter of the welle than of the tonne" (215). She stays busy – "She knew wel labour, but noon ydel ese" (217) and "She wolde noght been ydel til she slepte" (224), Chaucer remarks approvingly – and her industry is the sort necessary for living. There is no wasted motion with Griselda, no hunting and hawking, no "lust present". She is near to the fundamental stuff of life itself.

Griselda shows her affinity with Natura in her devotion to the bond of natural kinship. She is diligent in caring for Janicula, the person most closely bound to her by blood. He, her father, was Natura's agent in shaping her existence, and her ministrations to him express love which transcends mere affection: "And in reverence and charitee / Hir olde povre fader fostred shee" (221-222). Griselda's filial devotion is rather special. Essentially, it expresses her respect for Natura's sacred obligation to see that life continues from creature to creature, her reverence for Natura's life-giving powers. Janicula is her father; she loves and serves him because she is his child. For this simple and natural reason "ay she kepte hir fadres lyf on-lofte / With everich obeisaunce and diligence / That child may doon to fadres reverence" (229-231). Griselda's behavior toward Janicula prefigures but does not entirely explain her behavior toward Walter. After she marries him, he as her husband holds a station of utmost importance in Natura's scheme for human life. For this reason Griselda, bound by Natura's law to honor him, owes him love and reverence. Important here is the fact that in Griselda's love for Walter there are no overtones of the courtly love conventions. When Walter proposes and asks her obedience, she plights her troth without coyness or pretended scorn; when she marries him, she becomes his completely. Her quiet affirmations at the height of Walter's tyranny betray a quality of emotion foreign to the courtly heroine:

> "But certes, lord, for noon adversitee,
> To dyen in the cas, it shal nat bee
> That evere in word or werk I shal repente
> That I yow yaf myn herte in hool entente."   (858-861)

> "Ne nevere, for no wele ne no wo,
> Ne shal the goost withinne myn herte stente
> To love yow best with all my trewe entente."   (971-973)

Griselda does not serve "Venus ne Cupide". In bestowing love, she serves Natura, and her love, once given, is steadfast, enduring, and unchangeable.

In one vital trait, steadfastness, Griselda and Natura are at once alike and vastly different. Both are stable,[8] and in all that this characteristic implies, both are the antithesis of Walter and Fortuna. Walter's deeds are impulsive; Griselda's, predictable. Walter's behavior is fickle; hers, steadfast. More important, Walter's actions are often irrational, but Griselda's are always strongly motivated by love. For Griselda, as for Natura, this motivation forms the basis for her steadfastness. Natura's love encompasses all her living creatures, whom she has created, whom she fosters with her plenitude, and whom she prompts to continue the sacred work of propagation. Griselda loves those people to whom she is linked by Natura's sacred process of engendering and perpetuating life: her father, her husband, her children. In the intensity of her love for Walter, however, Griselda surpasses even the devotion of the goddess Natura and emerges not as a pale emanation of a cosmic force but as an enigmatic human character who transcends the pattern set by a lower deity and with almost superhuman humanity directly approaches a love like that of God. In steadfastness and enduring love, Natura finally has her limits: the whole of *De Planctu* is Natura's cosmic "grucch" against mankind; and as Natura oversees the fashioning of the new human being in *Anticlaudianus,* the work assumes her irritation with the mess man has made of himself. Natura has good reason for finding human beings objectionable, but the point is that she does complain. Griselda never does. Thus Chaucer once again indicates that Natura, just as Fortuna, is a limited deity, one whom human beings can, through human qualities, rise above. By balancing Natura and Griselda Chaucer portrays his heroine, who reacts with ultimate steadfastness, as reinforcing her human, rather than her allegorical, identity.[9] Walter, under the sway of Fortuna, from the beginning cannot endure the benign influence which Griselda brings to his realm.

[8]   *De Planctu: PL*, CCX. 293. 35-46. *Boece*, III. meter 2. E. C. Knowlton, "Nature in Old French", *MP*, XX (1923), 313, notes that Simond de Freine puts Fortune under Nature to show Fortune's instability.

[9]   Aldo D. Scaglione, *Nature and Love in the Late Middle Ages* (Berkeley, 1963) makes several references to the tradition of the Griselda-ideal of womanhood, "joyful, irrational obedience and total self-sacrifice" (p. 31) as opposed to the courtly ideal. See pp. 32, 52, 71, 74, 118.

In an effort to make her forfeit Natura's dominion over her by lapsing from stability and steadfastness, he inflicts upon her indignities which strike at the heart of her natural function as a woman: he deprives her of her son and daughter and denies her worthiness to bear his children. Griselda, however, refuses to capitulate, and, by her very refusal, she not only asserts Natura's principle of love and establishes her own spiritual inviolability, but she negates the hold of Fortuna upon Walter and his kingdom.

In the beginning of the tale Walter, charmed with the "favour of Fortune", refuses to recognize his natural responsibility as a mature human being: "And eek he nolde – and that was worst of alle – / Wedde no wyf, for noght that may bifalle" (83-84). In this refusal he denies his obligation to the law of kind and offends against Natura, the "vicaire of the almyghty Lord". As the spokesman of the delegation hints, he has not married because he cannot endure the possibility of servitude that marriage might bring; like Fortuna, he refuses to be bound. Ironically, he does not realize that he, with his seemingly carefree and dashing life, is less free than his poorest subject because he is so mastered by Fortuna that he is bound to her every whim.

Griselda from the first has a decidedly sobering effect upon Walter. When he sees her "paraventure", he is deeply charmed: "He noght with wantown lookyng of folye / His eyen caste on hire, but in sad wyse / Upon hir chiere he wolde hym ofte avyse" (236-238). The goddess of kind has wrought so wondrously in Griselda's creation that the sight of her takes aback even the scion of Fortuna. Her "yong age", "wommanhede", "vertu", and "bountee" are so overwhelming that Walter cannot resist them, and he begins secret marriage preparations. When he calls for her on the day of the wedding, her presence once again effects in him something of its own calm and quietude so that he becomes "thoghtful" and speaks to her about the marriage "ful sobrely". But he must remain master, for the darling of Fortuna does not thus meekly abdicate; thereby he extracts from Griselda a solemn oath of uncomplaining obedience to him. He has her stripped of her clothing and re-dressed, "for that no thyng of hir olde geere

/ She sholde brynge into his hous" (372-373). Walter does not intend that any external symbol of Griselda's innate devotion to Natura go with her to his palace. Thus the paragon of Natura marries the favorite of Fortuna.

At this point Walter seems to have the decided advantage. Griselda swears unquestioning obedience; she leaves her simple life, her sheep, her "wortes", her father; she becomes the marquess of Walter's "many a tour and toun"; she moves to Fortuna's own home ground. Walter lavishes upon her the glittering accoutrements of false felicity:

> ... this markys hath doon make
> Of gemmes, set in gold and in asure,
> Brooches and rynges, for Grisildis sake ...
> And eek of othere aornementes alle
> That unto swich a weddyng sholde falle.   (254-255; 258-259)

> A corone on hire heed they han ydressed,
> And sette hire ful of nowches grete and smale.   (381-382)

And yet the first triumph is Griselda's – and Natura's. Although to outward appearance Griselda is completely transformed – the people do not recognize her and her father thinks she is someone else – she does not become Fortuna's minion. Instead, her sudden rise on the fickle goddess's wheel enhances her basic humanity; the fine surroundings remove any too-realistic aromas of the "cote" and "oxes stalle" and show her inherent beauty and grace to their best advantage. Thus, she endears herself to the people:

> For though that evere vertuous was she,
> She was encressed in swich excellence
> Of thewes goode, yset in heigh bountee,
> And so discreet and fair of eloquence,
> So benigne and so digne of reverence,
> And koude so the peples herte embrace,
> That ech hire lovede that looked in hir face.   (407-413)

Because of her, the state prospers. She has an unusual knack for bringing order from chaos and harmony from disunity in affairs of governance. Even if there is trouble between "gentil men or othere" when Walter is away, she resolves the misunderstandings with great wisdom and discernment: "Ther nas discord, rancour, ne hevynesse / In al that land, that she ne koude apese, / And wisely brynge hem alle in reste and ese" (432-434). Griselda adds the steadying influence of Natura to Fortuna's improvident guidance, and the realm is the richer for her presence in the palace. The blessing of God is upon home and commonwealth as a result of Griselda's beneficent ministry. Walter lives "ful esily / At hoom" in the midst of the peace and plenty, and "outward grace ynogh had he" (424). But outward grace is as far removed from inward grace as false felicity is from true felicity. Walter has not changed with his changing realm, and for this reason the concord is short-lived. After the first child is born, Walter, as Fortuna's man, asserts his wilful dominion once more through the series of trials which he inflicts upon Griselda. Now instead of heaping her with worldly honors, he subjects her to adversity of the cruellest sort in an effort to force his own Fortune-controlled universe upon her. Walter's course of action in the testing episodes is monstrous and unnatural. The fact that he keeps the children safe is beside the point; his offense is in depriving Griselda of her natural function of motherhood. With his every move against Griselda he strikes a flagrant blow against Natura's sacred laws. Thomas R. Lounsbury vigorously insists that Griselda rather than Walter is the unnatural one: "Griselda fails in a woman's first duty, the defence of her offspring. She allows them to be sacrificed, as she supposes, without protest, to suit the whim of a ruthless father . . . . Griselda does not even exhibit the degree of sensibility which exists in the females of the brute creation." [10] By giving up her children in deference to Walter's wishes, Griselda is behaving neither like an animal nor like a goddess – Natura, who, as mentioned earlier, has limits of endurance, would not submit without protest to indignity against her offspring. Instead, Griselda is exercising purely human will and choice, with all the agony of spirit that such choice involves.[11] Her love for Walter is absolute, more absolute than Natura's for

---

[10]   *Studies in Chaucer,* III (New York, 1892), 340-341.
[11]   Donaldson, pp. 918-920, bases his view of Griselda on this point, without reference to Natura.

mankind; thus Chaucer asserts his faith in human qualities to bestow a love approaching the divine.

Griselda retains basic affinities with Natura in that the reactions of both exert a kind of cosmic force. In creating and fostering her world of natural creatures Natura exerts cosmic energy; for example, in Alain's *De Planctu* the natural world revives and blooms afresh when the goddess approaches. In one way this force seems passive: Natura is powerful in her creative love, but she is impotent to hate or to destroy. The lament of Alain's goddess in *De Planctu* springs not from hate for erring humankind but from thwarted love: she longs for man to live as part of her realm once more rather than desires to annihilate him for his base offenses against her laws. In the *Anticlaudianus* Alain does not show the fate of the old man before Natura, assisted by her handmaidens, creates a new and perfect human being.[12] And the goddess takes no part in the battle royal at the end of the *Anticlaudianus*.[13] But even more for Griselda than for Natura, creative love, her means of assertion, is also her means of defense. Griselda's resistance is not entirely passive. The forbearance and constancy of her passion safeguard her love against forces of open destruction and hate, and they also exert an active power for molding good from ill and amity from discord. Thus Griselda's "spinelessness" when her children are taken is basically not passive. She not only withstands but in her own way resists the onslaught of Walter: ultimately, Walter must bow before Griselda's love and acknowledge that this force, and not the fickleness of Fortuna, controls the universe. Each time the "ugly sergeant" comes, therefore, Griselda blesses her child, commends it to God, and, having surrendered it, lives as before, "evere in oon ylike sad and kynde" (602). She endures her deprivations with patience and cheerfulness: "As glad, as humble, as bisy in servyse, / And eek in love, as she was wont to be, / Was she to hym in every maner wyse" (603-605). Walter, at a loss to understand her unflagging devotion, almost suspects her

---

[12]   VII tells the creation of man and the gifts of the handmaidens (except for Fortuna, who is treated separately).

[13]   VIII. 337-369, IX. 1-409.

of nursing a grudge in secret. But Fortuna, not Natura, is master at dissimulation. And especially in Griselda, more stable than Natura, there is no guile.

Since Fortuna's vassal cannot budge Griselda from her steadfastness and constancy by taking her children from her, Walter aims the next indignity directly at the heart of her natural function by "divorcing" her as unfit to bear his children. This is an almost deadly blow, but

> . . . whan thise tidynges came to Grisildis,
> I deeme that hire herte was ful wo.
> But she, ylike sad for everemo,
> Disposed was, this humble creature,
> The adversitee of Fortune al t'endure.   (752-756)

Griselda is proof against the worst that Fortuna can do, and Walter's smug advice is superfluous: " 'No man may alwey han prosperitee. / With evene herte I rede yow t' endure / The strook of Fortune or of aventure' " (810-812). Like Alain's Natura she voices her plaint, regretting that Walter is not "kynde". Also like Alain's goddess, she laments that " 'love is noght oold as whan that it is newe' " (857): just as Venus grew bored with the unvarying happiness of her marriage with Vulcan and committed fornication with Antigamus, so Griselda is certain that Walter in his fickleness is tired of her. She goes away, stripped of everything she owns. She leaves with Walter all the jewels and rich garments which have been hers to enjoy and walks to her father's house practically naked. She is at the bottom of Fortuna's wheel. The people follow her weeping and cursing Fortuna; Janicula comes to meet her, weeping and cursing Natura.[14] These imprecations represent two extremes, both impossible for Griselda if she is to equal and surpass Natura's forbearance and constancy. She is the only character not thrown into a panic by Walter's capricious irrationality. She neither curses nor comments. She returns home, dressed, like Alain's Natura, in a torn mantle, and takes up her simple life again as cheerfully as though she had never left it. When Walter sees that she is out of his

---

[14]   The reference to Natura is not in the sources.

reach, her constancy unimpaired even by his latest abuse, he summons her again to the palace to undergo one final indignity.

Griselda's performance of her husband's final command strikes the telling blow not to her faith in love as the transcendent principle but to Fortuna's dominion over Walter. Instead of rebelling at this extremity of abuse or tearfully giving up, she carries out her duties of readying the house for Walter's new bride with "glad chiere" and executive skill. In her clothing "somdeel eek torent" she welcomes the girl and all the guests with genuine joy and praises her "with al hir herte, in ful benyngne entente" (1025). The climax comes as Walter summons Griselda before the company and asks "as it were in his pley, / 'How liketh thee my wyf and hire beautee?'" (1030-1031). This taunting question represents Walter's Fortune-dominated final effort to provoke Griselda into an uncharitable – and hence unnatural – response. Griselda, however, once again withstands, this time decisively. She not only speaks heartfelt praises for the girl but she shows deep concern for her welfare at Walter's hands. At this point Walter capitulates:

> And whan this Walter saugh hire pacience,
> Hir glade chiere, and no malice at al,
> And he so ofte had doon to hire offence,
> And she ay sad and constant as a wal,
> Continuynge evere hire innocence overal,
> This sturdy markys gan his herte dresse
> To rewen upon hire wyfly stedfastnesse.
>
> "This is ynogh, Grisilde myn", quod he.   (1044-1051)

He has assayed her "wommanheede", her "purpos", and her "wille" and found them faithful to Natura – and beyond – in every detail. He can do nothing else but surrender to Griselda's steadfast love. "Thus hath this pitous day a blisful ende" (1121), with festival more gladsome than at Griselda's marriage feast because the victory of love this time is permanent, not temporary. Here is a marked contrast with the first part of the poem. The people, who were split and factionalized by Walter's machinations to assert the dominance of his wilful unpredictability, live in harmony. Walter and Griselda live "in concord and in reste" (1129);

Janicula stays with them "in pees and reste" (1132); and their son finally rules "in reste and pees" (1136).

The purpose of this analysis has been to point out that on one level of interpretation Walter and Griselda reflect the traits of Fortuna and Natura and that they themselves depict in their conflict two extreme alternatives of reacting to the human situation. Chaucer focuses pertinent references in Petrarch and the French translator and effects innovations in his sources so that this conflict is present as a corollary to the main theme of Griselda's Christian patience. Every detail is basic; nothing is superfluous. There is no mention of Cupid, Venus, or courtly love; and there are no extended speeches on Boethian necessity or Christian charity. Chaucer focuses the action on a human scale; the characters are not stylizations of cosmic concepts. Though Walter and Griselda dramatize the difference between Fortuna's fickle tyranny and Natura's stable love, Chaucer clearly reveals that he does not regard either goddess as absolute. Walter's − and Fortuna's − shortcomings are obvious. Chaucer deals with Natura's more subtly, through Griselda, and establishes that Natura is not the antithetical good to Fortuna's ill. Griselda loves with a love that is more than natural − it is human; and in winning Walter to herself she portrays suggestions of the superhumanity of which man, through love, is capable.

IV. THE "KNIGHT'S TALE"

In the "Knight's Tale", Dame Natura and Dame Fortuna fit no neat pattern as they do in the two preceding discussions. Chaucer's use of Natura and Fortuna in this tale is complex and not easily definable. Here Chaucer does not consistently associate a particular deity with a particular character, as he does with Virginius, Virginia, Walter, and Griselda. Here, possibly because of the dominant strain of Boethianism he does not conceive of the characters as transcending Natura for a higher state of grace; here Natura leads one into the highest state of grace, into knowledge of God and acceptance of the universe. Fortuna and Natura – ultimately representing, as they do in the *Book of the Duchess*, death and reconciliation to life, respectively – act in sharp opposition throughout the tale in setting, character, and action and serve as thematic alternatives for the characters. There seems little point in a preliminary rehearsal of the myriad interpretations of the "Knight's Tale", since several competent scholars have reviewed the criticism.[1] The issues attendant upon philosophy, characterization, and the exact relation of the tale to its source are still matters for vigorous critical discussion.[2] This

---

[1] Paull F. Baum, *Chaucer: A Critical Appreciation* (Durham, 1958), pp. 99-100; E. B. Ham, *"Knight's Tale 38"*, *ELH*, XVII (1950), 252-261; A. H. Marckwardt, *Characterization in Chaucer's "Knight's Tale", University of Michigan Contributions in Modern Philology*, No. 5 (Ann Arbor, 1947), pp. 1-3.

[2] E. T. Donaldson, *Chaucer's Poetry* (New York, 1958), pp. 901-905; R. M. Lumiansky, *Of Sondry Folk* (Austin, 1955), pp. 29-49; Charles Muscatine, "Form, Texture, and Meaning in Chaucer's *Knight's Tale*", *PMLA*, LXV (1950), 911-929; R. A. Pratt, "Chaucer's Use of the *Teseida*",

study of Fortuna and Natura supports rather than negates a number of interpretations, especially those devoting attention to the Boethian philosophy in the tale. The goal here is to offer useful comments upon the functional role of the two Boethian semi-deities and their effect upon action, character, philosophy, and courtly love conventions in the "Knight's Tale".

A matter which deserves brief consideration is the importance of Natura and Fortuna in Chaucer's principal source, the *Teseida* of Boccaccio.[3] One striking feature of the *Teseida* is Boccaccio's constant use of epic machinery. Indeed, in Boccaccio's poem, the deities seem to have little function other than as epic agents. There are invocations to Mars (I. 3), Venus (I. 3), and the Muses (VIII. 2). Characters frequently swear by the deities, from Phoebus (IV. 75) to Mercury (X. 94), Vulcan (I. 91) to Juno (IV. 16). Besides the appearance of the gods in the heavenly quarrel scene, which Chaucer adapts for his own use, Mars enters directly into the action when he transfigures Teseo into his own likeness and encourages Arcita in the battle (VIII. 112-113). Fortuna, as frequently mentioned as any of the deities, also plays a conventional role. Usually Boccaccio uses "fortuna", the abstract concept – not Fortuna, the personification – and he employs it as a general term for luck, "sort", "aventure", or "cas". For example: " . . . con amaro / segno mostrar la fortuna nemica" (II. 15); " . . . e la mutata / fortuna trista di lieta tornata" (II. 37); " . . . quasi nel cor moriva di colore / per la fortuna sua" (III. 60); " . . . e mentre in dubbio fortuna . . . " (V. 33); " . . . sua fortuna angosciosa . . . " (IX. 21). In accordance with his view of the abstract concept, Boccaccio treats the goddess Fortuna as a personification of cosmic luck. She appears the essence

---

PMLA, LXII (1947), 601-617, and " 'Joye after wo' in the *Knight's Tale*", *JEGP*, XVII (1958), 416-423; Paul G. Ruggiers, "Some Philosophical Aspects of the *Knight's Tale*", *CE*, XIX (1958), 296-302; H. S. Wilson, "The *Knight's Tale* and the *Teseida* Again", *UTQ*, XVIII (1949), 131-146; Herbert G. Wright, *Boccaccio in England from Chaucer to Tennyson* (London, 1957), pp. 44-58.
[3] All references to Boccaccio are to *Teseida della Nozze d'Emilia*, ed. Aurelio Roncaglia (= *Scrittori d'Italia*, Vol. CLXXXV) (Bari, 1941).

of the traditional goddess, and Boccaccio adduces her blind and
fickle whim as the impelling force for the action:

> L'alta ministra del mondo Fortuna,
> con volubile moto permutando
> di questo in qual piú volte ciascheduna
> cosa togliendo e tal volta donando,
> or mostrandosi chiara e ora bruna
> secondo le pareva e come a quando . . . . (VI. 1)

The characters frequently lament her as the cause of their plights:
" 'O misera Fortuna de' viventi, / quanti dài moti spessi alle tue
cose!' " (IV. 80); " 'Ome, Fortuna dispietata e fella, / che t'ho io
fatto che si mi se' rea?' " (IV. 11); " 'tu [Amor] e la Fortuna / a tal
m'avete recata qui una' " (VIII. 96). On the surface, Boccaccio's
view of Fortuna resembles Chaucer's. The *Teseida*, however,
lacks the Boethian note which makes a happy ending a triumph
over the power of the goddess rather than a surprising gift from
the goddess's own fickle pleasure.

Since Fortuna holds undisputed sway, Boccaccio does not use
the goddess Natura as a counter-force to Fortuna's influence.
Indeed, the goddess Natura plays no part in Boccaccio's poem.
The abstract "natura" appears a few times, usually with a meaning equivalent to "human kind". Most of Boccaccio's nature
imagery seems to be of the conventional epic sort; for example,
to denote the passing of time:

> Il sole avea due volte dissolute
> le nevi en gli alti poggi, e altrettante
> Zeffiro aveva le frondi rendute
> e i be' fiori alle spogliate piante,
> poi che d'Attena s'eran dipartute
> le greche navi . . . . (II. 1)

Boccaccio uses natural imagery to describe the beauty of the
women, but this use also is conventional because he uses it for
everyone with equal enthusiasm. Emilia is "bella piu che fresca
rosa" (III. Argument). Ipolita "sembiava matutina stella / o
fresca rosa del mese di maggio" (I. 125). And the court ladies
are "belle, leggiadre, fresche e graziose" (I. 132). At least for
Ipolita, this imagery seems rather out of tone since Boccaccio

stresses that her role as a lady warrior is monstrous and sinful.

Thus the *Teseida* is permeated by a mysterious sense of whimsical fate which no mortal action can hope to brighten. Emilia feels strangely cursed by the gods (X. 68-75; XII. 39-42): because of their malevolence, she loses two lovers – Acate and Arcite – and she fears that marrying Palamon will mean his doom. Though Teseo pleads that all the characters accept the order of the universe, in which he sees some benevolence, the basis of his plea is not the mystical union of object with object through love. Instead, " 'sostenere / il piacer dell' iddii lieti dobbiamo, / poi ch'ad esso resister non possiamo' " (XII. 6). Boccaccio does not place the deities Natura and Fortuna in any sort of functional opposition.

To assert automatically that Chaucer has design where Boccaccio does not is impossible, but there seems to me basis for establishing a fundamental opposition between Natura and Fortuna in the "Knight's Tale". When Chaucer changes the scope of the poem from epic to romance, he does away with most of Boccaccio's conventional epic machinery. Yet he retains and even heightens the image of Fortuna, and he introduces the personification of Natura, who acts as a counter influence. Chaucer brings in Fortuna almost immediately, when he introduces Theseus.[4] He specifically mentions Natura and her cosmic significance near the end; first, when Arcite is dying (2758-2760), and second, when Theseus explains Boethian order in terms of the natural hierarchy (3007ff). There are numerous disquisitions on Fortuna throughout the tale, and at least one character (Arcite) bows to her as his controlling deity. There is implicit emphasis on Natura at every point in the narrative. Chaucer changes his source so that every major event occurs in the month of May, and he introduces the two Maying scenes of Emily (1034ff) and Arcite (1491ff). None of the characters in the poem is devoted wholly to Natura and none to Fortuna. Characters and kingdoms vacillate throughout the tale. The victory ultimately resides in the principles of Natura; but Natura's dominion over characters and

---

[4]   Lines 893ff. References to the "Knight's Tale" are to Fragment I.

kingdoms is an evolutionary process, not sudden, developing slowly and finding its expression only with the measured passage of time.

As a convenient beginning, I shall outline the significance of Fortuna and Natura in the setting and action of the tale, mentioning details which I shall discuss more fully later. A constant and carefully wrought tension between setting and action underlies the conflict between the two goddesses. Since Chaucer redesigns his source so that every major event occurs in Athens in the month of May, the setting consistently belongs to Natura. Emily's appearance in the garden, Arcite's ritualistic visit to the woods, the tourney for the hand of Emily – Chaucer creates the May background with definite intent. His purpose is to show the pristine freshness of every May scene, and by extension of Natura herself, violated by a series of Fortune-impelled events enacted by Fortune-motivated characters who are fundamentally out of harmony with the natural order. As I shall discuss shortly, Theseus is out of harmony as long as he acts with unpredictable inconsistency, one moment harsh and despotic, the next instant merciful and clement. The Fortune-crowned conqueror, he enters Athens after acting the cavalier despot in disposing of his prisoners; hence, the influence of the goddess enters the city with him. Palamon and Arcite, while they are in prison, negate the benign influence of the May season by giving in to despair of the sort Boethius felt at being abandoned by Fortuna. Arcite, losing all pretense of equanimity and Boethian acceptance, vows that release from prison means his death because he can no longer see Emily. Palamon, in jealousy over Arcite's love for Emily, loses interest in the natural world and, crying out against his prison for the first time, indulges in self-damning and futile invective over the injustice of Fortuna and the eternal order of a universe which demands that the innocent should suffer.

Most of the subsequent scenes take place in the one spot in the tale which most clearly belongs to the realm of Natura: the woods "a myle or tweye" from the Fortune-corrupted court of Athens, the grove which Arcite chooses as the perfect place to do honor to the Maytime. After Arcite's brief hymn of homage

in his Maying scene, Natura's grove undergoes repeated violation, first by the fighting knights and then by Theseus. Theseus
unwittingly acts as the agent of Fortuna in the wood on three
occasions. First, he there announces that he will award Emily in
marriage to the knight whom Fortuna favors with victory in a
tourney. Emily, a votaress of Natura, is promised as a prize for
Fortuna's champion; the grove where Theseus makes the pledge
belongs to Natura; and Arcite deserts his new allegiance to the
goddess to contend for Fortuna's victory. Second, Theseus de-
cides that the lists for the contest should stand in the grove. As
I shall discuss later, he also builds temples there, each an ambiguous combination of beauty and horror and each in its inconsistency bearing an implicit resemblance to the palace of Fortuna
in Alain's *Anticlaudianus*.[5] The contest in Natura's grove takes
place in the month of May. Here Fortuna awards victory to
Arcite and then suddenly tumbles him from her wheel. At the
end of the sequence, "Nature hath now no dominacioun" (2758);
thus, for the second time Fortuna wins in Natura's sylvan domain. Third, Theseus violates the grove with Arcite's funeral. In
doing honor to Arcite, Theseus unwittingly throws the glade into
pandemonium. Fortuna's victory is implicit, but indicated by the
extreme pomp of the funeral. The last scene of the tale, which
brings "joye after wo", takes place neither in the month of May
nor in the grove, but in an unspecified time of year in Theseus'
court. By changing time and setting in this manner, Chaucer
vividly reveals the pervasiveness of Natura's eventual triumph,
which comes with the passing of grief and the growth of understanding in Theseus, Palamon, and Emily. At the end of the
tale, Natura's beneficence is no longer confined by season or
geography; rather, it is timeless, penetrating to every corner of
the kingdom.

With this tension between setting and action constantly in the
background, Chaucer develops the opposition between the concepts of Fortuna and Natura in varying complexity in the four
principal characters. The character of Theseus typifies the op-

[5] VII. 405-480.

position. Critics agree that Chaucer effects a striking and puzzling change when he adapts the character of Teseo to his own "Knight's Tale". Boccaccio's Teseo is consistently the noble ruler, acting with equanimity and wisdom on every occasion.[6] Chaucer's Theseus is a character of extremes – gentle or arrogant, unpredictably exacting or mild in command, whimsically stringent or clement in judgment.[7] A number of scholars believe that Theseus is the representative of the Boethian Destiny which controls the tale.[8] In my opinion, Theseus is not in command of the Boethian Destiny which operates in the tale; rather, he, like all the other characters, falls under the sway of Destiny's agents. While Fortuna influences Theseus, his domain – victorious Athens and conquered Thebes – is in vague unrest. When Theseus reaches an acceptance of Boethian order, the kingdoms of Athens and Thebes unite and there is universal concord. Further, Theseus is not, as most critics regard him, a static figure. His character follows a definite line of development as he rises above the tyranny of Fortuna to an acceptance of the ordered love of Natura, as he grows from a dim and inarticulate understanding of the universe to a more perfect comprehension which finds its fluent expression in the power, wisdom, and beauty of his bond-of-love oration. In short, Theseus grows from the power of action to the more philosophically profound power of speech.

At three points in the narrative Chaucer links Fortuna, Destiny, and Natura with the actions of Theseus. At his first appearance, Chaucer associates Theseus with Fortuna (915ff); midway through the tale, Chaucer points out that Theseus is ruled by Boethian Destiny (1663ff); and at the end of the tale, Chaucer establishes the lordship of Natura over the duke

---

[6] For a typical description, see Pratt, "Chaucer's Use of the *Teseida*", p. 602.

[7] For a sharp indictment of Chaucer's treatment, see Wright, pp. 46-47. H. J. Webb, "A Reinterpretation of Chaucer's Theseus", *RES*, XXIII (1947), 289-296, examines possible reasons for the extremes in Theseus' character.

[8] See, for example, Bernhard ten Brink, *History of English Literature*, II (London, 1901), 70; William A. Frost, "An Interpretation of Chaucer's *Knight's Tale*", *RES*, XXV (1949), 297; Muscatine, p. 922; Baum, p. 97.

(2987ff). In the figure of Theseus, Chaucer keeps the background clash between Fortuna and Natura visible. Chaucer's Theseus is much like Boccaccio's Teseo. Chaucer calls him "this gentil duc / . . . with herte pitous" (952-953), who rescinds an impulsive death decree because "pitee renneth soone in gentil herte" (1761). But Theseus is most aptly characterized by his herald, who declares, "He wol his firste purpos modifye" (2542). At no time until the end of the tale does Theseus make a single decision and stick by it. Whenever he makes a decree, he invariably changes his mind and, significantly, changes it in matters dealing with life and sudden death. Theseus makes his entrance under the powerful aegis of Lady Fortune. He appears on the road to Athens "with victorie and with melodye" (872), surrounded by the booty of his conquests – a humbled queen, a princess, "and al his hoost in armes hym bisyde" (874). He rides "in al his wele and in his mooste pride" (895); he is the " 'Lord, to whom Fortune hath yiven / Victorie, and as a conqueror to lyven' " (915-916). From the mastery of Fortuna over him comes the seeming inconsistency in his character. While he bows to Fortune, he is stern, rash, hasty, and impulsive; he delights in the glitter of false felicity; he appears before his people "arrayed right as he were a god in trone" (2529). He intends to be " 'a rightful lord and juge' " (1719) and an " 'evene juge . . . and trewe' " (1864); but the clashing paradox of Fortuna and Natura within him prevents him from consistency of action or speech.

When the forlorn "compaignye of ladyes, tweye and tweye, / Ech after oother, clad in clothes blake" (898-899) stops Theseus on his way home to Athens, his first impulse toward them is callous because the outcry mars the grandeur of this triumphant march:

> "What folk been ye, that at myn homcomynge
> Perturben so my feste with criynge?"
> Quod Theseus. "Have ye so greet envye
> Of myn honour, that thus compleyne and crye?"   (905-908)

But suddenly, unpredictably, he loses his sternness, and he addresses them in his role as righteous champion of justice: " 'Or who hath yow mysboden or offended? / And telleth me if it may been amended, / And why that ye been clothed thus in blak'" (909-911). In his role of sympathetic defender, he avenges their grief by conquering Creon and Thebes and allowing the women to bury their dead. With knightly sympathy he accepts their cause as his own and does them great honor.

This early encounter sets the pattern for Theseus' reaction to all major events in the tale: an immediate exhibition of sternness, not to say harshness, followed by an equally sudden display of clemency and mercy. When the "pilours" discover Palamon and Arcite after the battle at Thebes, they treat the two knights with more consideration than does Theseus: they remove them from the heap of bodies "and han hem carried softe unto the tente / Of Theseus" (1021-1022). And Theseus "ful soone hem sente / To Atthenes, to dwellen in prisoun / Perpetuelly, – he nolde no ransoun" (1022-1024). Apparently without a moment's deliberation he disposes of Arcite and Palamon in a cavalier fashion worthy of Dame Fortuna herself.[9] Chaucer sets the lord and the vanquished in painful contrast. Theseus returns to Athens

> With laurer crowned as a conquerour;
> And ther he lyveth in joye and in honour
> Terme of his lyf; what nedeth wordes mo?
> And in a tour, in angwissh and in wo,
> This Palamon and his felawe Arcite
> For everemoore; ther may no gold hem quite.   (1027-1032)

"This passeth yeer by yeer and day by day" (1033); then Theseus unpredictably softens his stand. Prevailed upon by Perotheus, he dismisses the ransom entirely and liberates Arcite "frely to goon wher that hym liste over al" (1207). He does exile the knight, but under ordinary circumstances – if Arcite were not in love with Emily – exile would work no hardship upon the released prisoner. That Theseus does not release Palamon also is not particularly significant; Palamon has no champion and his imprisonment is necessary for the plot. Theseus' sudden gesture of clemency is the important action.

9   In the *Teseida* (II. 99), Teseo treats Palamon and Arcita with every consideration in prison "perche di sangue reale eran nati".

Theseus repeats these reactions at his next appearance, when Boethian Destiny impels him to go hunting in the woods and he finds Palamon and Arcite fighting. When he comes upon the battling knights, he impetuously rushes between them and threatens them with death if they lift their swords to strike. When Palamon blurts out their identity, Theseus instantly pronounces a death sentence upon them (1743ff). But once again he is not consistent. When the queen, Emily, and the court ladies raise an outcry in behalf of the two condemned knights, Theseus does a complete about-face by forgiving them both outright. Chaucer carefully traces Theseus' mood from rage (1762) to reason (1765ff) to compassion (1770-1771). Ultimately Theseus chides himself roundly for his cruel impulse: " 'Fy / Upon a lord that wol have no mercy . . . ' " (1773-4). Here Chaucer shows Theseus awakening to forces of Nature within him which demand that he respect life, not regard it as worthless.[10] His lightly ironic oration to the god of love, with which he prefaces his forgiveness and offer of friendship, emphasizes his growing tolerance: he finds the muddled triangle both understandable and delightful, not contemptible or ridiculous. In his new regard for Arcite and Palamon as fellow human beings, Theseus is moved to give them both a fair chance to win the hand of Emily.

When he attempts to find a solution for the love dilemma, however, he turns the resolution over to Fortuna by proposing a bloody contest, with Fortuna to decide the victor:

> "Thanne shal I yeve Emelya to wyve
> To whom that Fortune yeveth so fair a grace."   (1860-1861)

> "Ye shul noon oother ende with me maken,
> That oon of yow ne shal be deed or taken."   (1865-1866)

He pursues his grim intent as he builds the lists and the temples.

---

[10] Compassion is not an attribute of Fortuna. And Reason, except in matters of love, is often the handmaiden of Natura. See, for example, *Anticlaudianus*, II. 1-157. Also see Boethius' *De Consolatione*, in which Lady Philosophy leads Boethius to acceptance through the processes of reason.

Commissioned in honor of the contest which Fortuna is to arbitrate, each of the temples – like the palace of Fortuna in the *Anticlaudianus* [11] – presents a strange and incongruous picture. Each temple is wrought expensively (Theseus "at his grete cost arrayed thus / The temples" – 2090-2091; and Mars' shrine alone "coste largely of gold a fother" – 1908) and exquisitely (Diana's temple is made of "alabastre whit and reed coral" – 1910; and all three contain "noble kervyng" and "portreitures" – 1915). In each shrine the statue of the deity is noble and majestic; but the frescoes of the temples are filled with terrors, both subtle and explicit: "The broken slepes, and the sikes colde ..." (1920); "The colde deeth, with mouth gapyng upright" (2008); "A womman travaillynge ... / But for hir child so longe was unborn" (2083-2084). In creating such extremes, with each deity a picture of wondrous majesty and each temple a gallery of horrors, Chaucer approaches the method of Alain of Lille in his handling of the fickle goddess. Thus Chaucer indicates the controlling hand of Fortuna in Theseus' construction of the lists and the temples.

On the day of the tourney, when Theseus faces the issue of making a game of human slaughter, he cannot act upon his impulsive edict of a year ago. He impetuously orders the tournament rules revised so that the combatants will have almost no chance of killing each other (2537ff): Theseus, the now-beneficent ruler, acts in accord with beneficent Natura. Neither Natura nor the warriors is responsible for Arcite's mortal wound by the "furie infernal". For this reason, Theseus, still the gracious lord, refuses to regard the tragic event as more than a minor mishap or to let it spoil the holiday of the visiting knights.

When Arcite dies, Theseus' allegiance to Natura fails once more. He grieves out of measure until his father – whom I shall discuss later – offers him consolation. Egeus' speech summarizes succinctly the ordered course of events in the natural world and gives Theseus the background for acceptance of a universe ordered by divine necessity rather than by blind chance. Yet at

[11]   See VII. 405-480; VIII. 1-62.

this moment Egeus' counsel does not penetrate Theseus' under-standing. The words of his father suffice to stop his immediate grief, but Theseus does not pause to consider their import. In-stead, "with al his bisy cure" (2853), Theseus considers how best to honor the dead knight. He chooses the grove, "swoote and grene" (2860), as the spot for Arcite's funeral because there he first discovered Arcite's passion for Emily; and he acts with the best intention of paying homage to Arcite and his devoted love in the place where Arcite "hadde his amorouse desires, / His compleynte, and for love his hoote fires" (2861-2862). Theseus' tribute to Arcite in the grove honors the Theban warrior – and hence Fortuna, who elevated Arcite and tumbled him from her wheel – but it also wreaks destruction upon Natura's domain. Egeus tells Theseus to accept death as part of the natural order:

> "Right as ther dyed nevere man", quod he,
> "That he ne lyvede in erthe in some degree,
> Right so ther lyvede never man", he seyde,
> "In al this world, that som tyme he ne deyde."   (2843-2846)

Theseus, acting contrary to Egeus' counsel, not only surrounds Arcite's death with extreme pomp and ceremony, but for his materials he plunders Natura's grove, tranquil and venerable with age. The "okes olde" (2866) and many other trees ("ook, firre, birch, aspe, alder, holm, popler, / Wylugh, elm, plane, assh, box, chasteyn, lynde, laurer, / Mapul, thorn, bech, hasel, ew, whippeltree" – 2921-2923) fall for the funeral pyre. The wood-land deities lose their homes:

> ... the goddes ronnen up and doun,
> Disherited of hire habitacioun,
> In which they woneden in reste and pees,
> Nymphes, fawnes and amadrides ....   (2925-2928)

The forest animals run in terror: " ... the beestes and the briddes alle / Fledden for fere, whan the wode was falle" (2929-2930). The pomp of the funeral pyre is a sacrilege to the earth of which Arcite again becomes a part: " ... the ground agast was of the light, / That was nat wont to seen the sonne bright" (2931-2932). Thus Theseus, in attempting to honor Arcite, unwittingly uses nature in a perverted manner and throws the entire natural order askew. Chaucer uses this dramatic means to show that Theseus at this moment is not attuned to Natura's laws, and he presents the scene in vivid contrast to Theseus' next appearance, when he makes his bond-of-love oration.

In order for Natura's victory over the kingdom to be unmistakable, Theseus as the ruler must define his philosophical position. Throughout the tale, Theseus 1) acts silently in accord with Natura's law ("withouten moore abood, / His baner he desplayeth, and forth rood / To Thebes-ward" – 965-967); 2) lightly glosses his merciful actions (" 'The god of love, a *benedicite!* " – 1785); and 3) deputes to a herald an explanation for his clemency (" 'Wherfore, to shapen that they shal nat dye, / He wol his firste purpos modifye' " – 2541-2542). In his final speech, Theseus proves himself in perfect harmony with the laws of Natura and of the First Mover. Chaucer reveals him in the maturity of his understanding as he expands the terse comments of Egeus into a powerful and moving explanation of the divine love which orders the eternal mutability of nature.

Emily's significance arises from her simplicity, and, lest overemphasis give her disproportionate importance, I shall discuss her rather briefly. Her function in the tale is essential, and to fill this function Chaucer re-creates her from her prototype in the *Teseida*. Critics universally state that Chaucer's Emily resembles Boccaccio's Emilia in name only.[12] From Boccaccio's vividly drawn character who is fully aware of herself as a woman and who takes a major role in the action, Chaucer molds a charming, silent and shadowy figure who impels the action through unconscious influence rather than through action. The customary explanation for Chaucer's de-emphasis of Emily is that it throws the contrast between the two knights into sharper focus. It seems to me that Chaucer has an additional reason for

---

[12]   G. F. Coulton, *Chaucer and His England*, 4th ed. (London, 1927), p. 222; William G. Dodd, *Courtly Love in Chaucer and Gower* (Gloucester, Mass., 1913), p. 239; J. R. Hulbert, "What Was Chaucer's Aim in the *Knight's Tale?*", *SP*, XXVI (1929), 375; Pratt, "Chaucer's Use of the *Teseida*", p. 602; R. K. Root, *The Poetry of Chaucer* (New York, 1906), p. 171; Wright, p. 49.

treating Emily as he does: he makes her the standard by which he measures Fortuna's pervasive influence. Emily begins and ends the tale as a votaress of Natura. Never does she falter in her loyalty to the goddess, but even she is swayed by the favor of Fortuna, so that her allegiance becomes a perversion of service to Natura. Thus, Chaucer emphasizes the power of Fortuna by showing that even Emily is affected by the vagaries of the fickle goddess.

In the beginning of the tale, Emily – as her very conventionality indicates – is the epitome of innocence, freshness, and purity:

> ... Emelye, that fairer was to sene
> Than is the lylie upon his stalke grene,
> And fressher than the May with floures newe –
> For with the rose colour stroof hire hewe,
> I noot which was the fyner of hem two – ....   (1035-1039)

When she appears, she – unlike Emilia, who frequently stages a little performance for Palamon and Arcite – is completely unselfconscious. A creature of Natura, she acts with instinctive enthusiasm in honoring May,

> For May wole have no slogardie a-nyght.
> The sesoun priketh every gentil herte,
> And maketh hym out of his slep to sterte,
> And seith "Arys, and do thyn observaunce".
> This maked Emelyne have remembraunce
> To doon honour to May, and for to ryse.   (1042-1047)

She watches the sunrise, gathers flowers, makes a garland, and sings, artlessly concerned with nothing but the joy of the season. Absorbed in her Maying, Emily never realizes the presence of the two watching knights.

When she abruptly becomes aware that she is the cause for the contention between the two knights "that foughten breme, as it were bores two" (1699), she reaffirms her loyalty to Natura by worshipping at the shrine of Diana. This pagan goddess has certain associations with Natura.[13] Like Natura, she is a deity of

---

[13] Walter Clyde Curry, *Chaucer and the Medieval Sciences* (New York, 1926), pp. 155ff, regards the planets and the gods which rule them as the agents of Fortuna. In general, I think this view is correct, especially

the outdoors. Like Natura, she is chaste, but she does not demand chastity of her subjects. She is goddess not only of chastity but also of childbirth. But Diana is not quite the same as Natura: for example, Diana is patroness of hunting, an activity destructive to the natural world. Chaucer treats her, like Venus, as a deity of double – or ambiguous – aspect. In the temple which Theseus commissions, the goddess herself is closely associated with the creatures and phenomena of the world of nature. She sits upon a hart; small hounds run about her; she is clothed in "gaude grene"; a waxing moon is beneath her feet. But she carries her deadly hunting gear, and she looks down into the realm of the dead, "Ther Pluto hath his derke regioun" (2082). The frescoes and adornments of the shrine illustrate this ambiguous relationship between Diana and the natural world. Taken chiefly from Ovid's *Metamorphoses*, they depict Diana's transformations of people (Callisto, Daphne, Actaeon, Meleager) into natural phenomena. However justified the goddess' vengeance, the result for her victims is not eternal peace as part of the natural universe. More often, it is dire calamity. For example:

Ther saugh I Attheon an hert ymaked,
For vengeaunce that he saugh Diane al naked;
I saugh how that his houndes have hym caught
And freeten hym, for that they knewe hym naught. (2065-2068)

Even the picture of Diana in the aspect of her deity wherein she most resembles Natura – goddess of childbirth – contrasts the depths of human suffering with the lack of divine compassion (2083-2086).

Though Diana's temple is ambiguous, Emily's orison is not: she plainly states that she intends to serve Diana as a maid. At this point, Emily, ostensibly serving Diana, is charmed with the "unnatural" aspects of the goddess' deity. She loves hunting and

---

for gods such as Mars and Mercury. In this tale, even though Venus appears in the heavenly quarrel scene, Chaucer indicates clearly that she can be linked with Fortuna or Natura. Further, Chaucer does not introduce Diana into the quarrel scene, thus placing her outside the strife of the Olympian agents of Fortuna and associating her, by implication, with Natura.

her life of freedom. Because she is carefree she does not want to take her place in Natura's world as a perpetrator of life:

> " . . . nevere wol I be no love ne wyf.
> I am, thow woost, yet of thy compaignye,
> A mayde, and love huntynge and venerye,
> And for to walken in the wodes wilde,
> And noght to ben a wyf and be with childe." (2306-2310)

She shows obedience to Natura in agreeing to marry if Destiny commands. Destiny does command: Natura intends human kind to carry on the species. Thus, Emily accepts the decree of Destiny delivered by Diana that she must wed one of the two knights. At the crucial moment, she confuses Fortuna and destiny. When Palamon is vanquished in the tourney she considers Arcite her betrothed: "And she agayn hym caste a freendlich ye / (For wommen, as to speken in comune, / Thei folwen alle the favour of Fortune)" (2680-2682). After he dies, she mourns for him as though he had been her husband, thus preventing the will of Natura and the decree of Destiny (that she marry Palamon) from coming to pass. Not until Theseus calls Palamon and Emily before him and wins them with his bond-of-love oration does Emily accept Destiny. Because of Theseus' speech, Emily sees her role in the natural order, and – unlike Boccaccio's Emilia – she agrees happily and without a word of protest to marry Palamon.

Just as Palamon and Arcite are sharply different in terms of Boethian philosophy, so they are different in the impact of Fortuna and Natura upon them.[14] Arcite dies because of Fortuna; Palamon attains worldly bliss when he accepts Natura's beneficently ordered universe. The complications which Palamon's character presents are basic to Chaucer's concept of Fortuna and Natura. With Palamon we see most vividly one of Chaucer's primary concerns in the tale: the difficult position of Venus and love in the conflict between Fortuna and Natura. The relationship between Venus and the two semi-deities does not enter into the "Clerk's Tale" and the "Physician's Tale", but it assumes

---

[14] For a summary of critical views of the two knights, see Marckwardt, pp. 1-3. For more recent studies, see especially Lumiansky, *Of Sondry Folk*, and Ruggiers.

great importance when Chaucer introduces courtly love.[15] Chaucer adopts something of the ambiguity of Alain of Lille towards Venus, tempering Alain's view to fit the courtly love situation. In *De Planctu Naturae*, Alain of Lille clearly has a dual attitude toward the goddess of love. Alain lifts the goddess from pagan mythology to make her a servant of Natura in the divine work of creation.[16] Natura herself is chaste. Thus she delegates Venus and her husband Vulcan as the divine agents of generation. When Venus commits adultery with Antigamus, she perverts her sacred office and paves the way for untold moral ills among humanity, but her work of propagating the species is still vital to God's plan. Venus is necessary, yet dangerous and reprehensible. Alain of Lille is concerned with one specific perversion of Venus, immorality in the monasteries, which he condemns. Despite Natura's sermon against Cupid, Alain cannot condemn the aspect of Venus which represents the human love necessary for God's design for man. Alain solves the problem by giving Venus a dual nature and by referring to her as "Venus in Venerem pugnans", at best a necessary evil.[17] Chaucer's attitude resembles Alain's in nothing but the duality. He never regards love with contempt, as does Alain, and he is never hard on Venus except by implication. For instance, in the *Parliament of Fowls*, Natura, not Venus, emerges as the ascendant figure. If the formel eagle is judging a contest between the two goddesses, she chooses Natura the winner. Yet Chaucer describes the garden of Venus with vitality. In the "Knight's Tale", Chaucer's ambiguous attitude toward Venus

---

[15] For general background on courtly love, without specific reference to Natura and Fortuna, valuable works are those by Dodd, especially pp. 1-37, 235-246; and Thomas A. Kirby, *Chaucer's Troilus: A Study in Courtly Love* (Baton Rouge, 1940), especially pp. 14-87.

[16] For philosophical background on Natura and Love, see Eugene Edward Slaughter, *Virtue According to Love – in Chaucer* (New York, 1957), pp. 107-123. For a discussion of Venus' relation to Natura in Alain and other authors, see E. C. Knowlton, "The Goddess Natura in Early Periods", *JEGP*, XIX (1920), 224-253; Richard Hamilton Green, "Alain of Lille's *De Planctu Naturae*", *Speculum*, XXXI (1956), 649-674.

[17] *PL*, CCX. 281.5. The concept of Venus' duality in *De Planctu* is discussed in Green, pp. 660-674.

and her relation to Natura and Fortuna takes dramatic form in the character of Palamon.

Palamon does not speak until after he sees Emily; thus, love influences virtually his every action in the tale. Chaucer emphasizes at Palamon's first appearance that the knight loves life. When Theseus throws him into prison, he is far from happy, but he does not, like Arcite, sink into apathy. Though physically removed from the world, he stays as close to life as he can. He habitually paces in a lofty room where the flux and bustle of the outside world are visible, where he can see "al the noble citee ..., / And eek the gardyn, ful of braunches grene" (1066-1067). He retains an affinity with the world of Natura and the world of man. The appearance of Emily in the garden presents him with another dimension of life: love. Significantly, he accepts love as a positive power for good as he makes his first prayer to Venus:

> ... "Venus, if it be thy wil
> Yow in this gardyn thus to transfigure
> Bifore me, sorweful, wrecched creature,
> Out of this prisoun help that we may scapen.
> And if so be my destynee be shapen
> By eterne word to dyen in prisoun,
> Of oure lynage have som compassioun,
> That is so lowe ybroght by tirannye."   (1104-1111)

The striking notes of this prayer are, first, its selflessness, and, second, its cheerful acceptance of destiny. "Help us" – not *me* – "to escape", and "Have compassion on our line" – not on *me* or on *my* line – he petitions. And at this point he accepts life imprisonment as a matter of course, if "eterne word" so decrees. To recapitulate: at his first appearance Palamon, though in prison, maintains a measure of harmony with Natura's universe, accepting his fate and regarding Venus as a benevolent agent of Destiny. Here he, rather than Arcite, shows the more valid philosophical solution because Palamon's acceptance springs directly from his way of life in prison.

When Arcite, too, sees Emily, Palamon's balance is unsettled. With the appearance of a rival in love, Palamon loses his equanimity: he looks "dispitously" (1124); he "knytte[s] his browes tweye" (1128); he takes Arcite to task, repeatedly calling him "fals" (1130, 1142, 1145, 1151). In short, he becomes jealous, and with jealousy enters all the machinery of the courtly love code. Palamon and Arcite argue incessantly and uselessly over love. In their debilitating strife Palamon loses his first apprehension of Venus as a natural part of God's ordered universe. With Arcite, he regards her instead as a deity with power over life and death, dominated by the whim of fickle Fortuna: " 'Thyn is the victorie of this aventure. / . . . Wel hath Fortune yturned thee the dys' " (1235, 1238), Arcite tells Palamon. In the "Knight's Tale" as generally, Chaucer effects a close correspondence between courtly love and the aspect of Venus which is ruled by Fortuna. He equates courtly love, though not the passion of love itself, with false felicity. When Palamon becomes embroiled in the artificial conventions surrounding the goddess of love, when his bickering with Arcite about the merits of prison and release causes the narrator to phrase a stereotyped and conventional *demande d'amour*, Palamon is ruled by "ars magicae Veneris".[18] He is wholly prey to Fortuna. Riddled with jealousy, Palamon at this point – but not before this point – is in a state of mind analogous to that of Boethius at the beginning of his imprisonment. Thus he inveighs against Fortuna (1303-1308), the hierarchy of the gods (1328-1329), the mortal power of Venus (1332-1333), and the benevolent order in the universe (1313-1314). This speech provides a marked contrast to his first humble prayer to Venus.

When Palamon escapes prison "by aventure or destynee" (1465), he acts as Fortuna's pawn to bring Arcite into the fickle goddess' snare (1490). Palamon, like Arcite, is "Now up, now doun, as boket in a welle" (1533), because of love and the influence of "geery Venus" (1536). For this reason, he provokes the battle over Emily, which Theseus interrupts when he is drawn to the scene by Destiny. When Theseus stops the fight, Palamon plays Fortuna's minion in asking immediate death for himself

---

[18] Alain's phrase for the craft of the perverted Venus – *De Planctu*: *PL*, CCX. 281.18.

and his rival, in attempting to subject them both to the final indignity of Fortuna: "'Wherfore I axe deeth and my juwise; / But sle my felawe in the same wise, / For bothe han we deserved to be slayn'" (1739-1741). This sort of pleading is much different from the courtly love talk of wounds and death by Cupid's arrows and the eyes of the beloved. As with the birds in the *Parliament*, the courtly jargon represents a basic wish, however inverted its expression, for life, a longing for the realm of Natura but mistakenly addressed. Here Palamon, seriously asking for death, suggests the resolution most abhorrent to Natura and, by implication, most satisfactory to Fortuna.

Chaucer presents his concept of Venus as a dual deity most vividly in the scenes in Venus' temple. The temple which Theseus commissions is a shrine to the unstable, kaleidoscopic goddess of the courtly love tradition. The statue of Venus represents a strange mixture of the natural and the artificial: doves fly above her; roses deck her hair, but the waves from which she rises are not like water but as "brighte as any glas" (1958). Cupid, a stock figure in courtly tradition, appears a stereotyped picture ("as it is often seene" – 1965), with his blind eyes and his deadly bow and arrows. Chaucer gives a faintly poisonous quality to the rich artistry of the temple. Rather than depicting the joys of love, the shrine portrays the ills and unhappiness attendant upon the lover's malady:

> The broken slepes and the sikes colde,
> The sacred teeris, and the waymentynge,
> The firy strokes of the desirynge
> That loves servantz in this lyf enduren.   (1920-1923)

The personifications "wroght on the wal" are an ambiguous mixture of pleasantry and venial sin – the sugar-plum delights of false felicity:

> Plesaunce and Hope, Desir, Foolhardynesse
> Beautee and Youthe, Bauderie, Richesse,
> Charmes and Force, Lesynges, Flaterye,
> Despense, Bisynesse, and Jalousye .... (1925-1928)

The array of historical and mythical personages illustrates the perversion (Narcissus – 1941) and the folly (Solomon – 1942 –

and Croesus – 1946) to which doting lovers are victim when they serve the inconstant Venus.

Palamon's petition, which he makes in this shrine, bears virtually no relation to his frescoed surroundings. Guided by Natura's harbinger of day, the lark (2210), he is filled with reverence and confidence in his purpose – "with hooly herte and with an heigh corage" (2213), "with humble cheere / And herte soor" (2219-2220); thus he addresses this prayer as he did his first, not to the Venus of courtly convention, but to the handmaiden of Natura. He prays to Venus in her divine station as wife to Vulcan (2222). His promise to " 'holden werre alwey with chastitee' " (2236) is directed only against Emily (" 'I wolde have fully possesioun / Of Emelye' " – 2242-2243) and is quite in accord with Natura's strictest principles in *De Planctu* and the *Roman*, disapproval of chastity and hatred of unnatural lust. Though Palamon mentions Venus and Adonis, the point of his allusion is Venus' grief at Adonis' death: just as the gods pitied and helped her, so she should pity and help him to save him from such sorrow. He does not mention Cupid, and he makes no use of the rhetorical conventions of courtly love:

> ". . . taak myn humble preyere at thyn herte.
> Allas! I ne have no langage to telle
> Th' effectes ne the tormentz of myn helle;
> Myn herte may myne harmes nat biwreye;
> I am so confus that I kan noght seye
> But, 'Mercy, lady bright' . . . ."   (2226-2231)

His prayer emerges as a straightforward, humble petition to a deity powerful in the natural order of the universe.

Though Palamon fights under the aegis of Venus, the battle itself is not of direct concern. When Arcite is mortally wounded by the Fury, Palamon's preoccupation with Venus recedes to the background as the knight is faced with the death of his friend. Arcite on his deathbed catches a glimpse of Palamon as Palamon longs to be – constant and devoted in Venus' service. Thus Arcite recommends him to Emily as a man most "worthy to ben loved" (2794). After Arcite dies, Palamon negates the healing power of Natura by grieving overmuch, just as Alcyone does in the *Book of the Duchess*. He continues his mourning after "al stynted is the moornynge and the teres / Of Grekes" (2968-2969), and he comes to Theseus' parliament "in his blake clothes sorwefully" (2978). But Theseus with his bond-of-love speech restores Palamon to a balanced view and resolves all difficulties with Venus, Fortuna, and Natura. Theseus' exposition of the natural order precludes the "geery Venus", since Theseus' precepts are based on the "parfit" and stable ordinances of the First Mover. At last, as the precepts of Natura win, so the "unfallen" Venus wins; and Palamon and Emily live in perfect harmony ("in blisse, in richesse, and in heele" – 3102), with no hint of courtly conventions to mar their love.

As the criticism dealing with him indicates, Arcite is a complicated character. He alone of the persons in the narrative moves from apparent acceptance to rebellion and despair; he moves from the protection of adherence to Natura to the malevolent destruction of Fortuna; he moves from life to death. After Arcite flies to pieces at his first sight of Emily, his problem is not to recover a spirit of philosophical calm from which he is temporarily jolted but to achieve a calm and quietude which he never really possessed. He fails; Chaucer gives clear indication that Arcite allows himself to be defeated by Fortuna, and at his end there can be no great surprise in Chaucer's resigned observation, "Nature hath now no dominacioun. / And certeinly, ther Nature wol nat wirche, / Fare wel phisik! go ber the man to chirche!" (2758-2760). Arcite provides the negative example of what, in my opinion, is a major philosophical tenet of the tale – that true Boethian acceptance is the reward of years and understanding. Arcite is Chaucer's vivid comment upon the "fugitive and cloistered virtue".

The first glimpse of Arcite and Palamon in prison is significant, for Chaucer sets them in attitudes characteristic of the years and days which have passed. Palamon walks aloft to look at the countryside and the garden ("As was his wone" – 1064), while Arcite sits in the cell. Thus, even before Arcite speaks, we have a definite hint that his attitude towards life is not that of a creature fully alive. His reaction to Palamon's cry at the sight of

Emily reveals the rift which Arcite has put between himself and the living world. When Palamon cries "A!" Arcite "anon up sterte" (1080), not to look upon the cause of his friend's exclamation, but to chide him for crying out against his prisoner's lot, lecturing him to endure what cannot be changed (1081-1085). He cites the disastrous caprice of Fortuna and the eternal mandate of the stars to convince Palamon of the futility of wishing to brighten their condition:

> "Fortune hath yeven us this adversitee.
> Som wikke aspect or disposicioun
> Of Saturne, by som constellacioun,
> Hath yeven us this, although we hadde it sworn;
> So stood the hevene whan that we were born.
> We moste endure it; this is the short and playn." (1086-1091)

In his effort to stamp out hope for himself and Palamon, Arcite completely misses the point of his friend's exclamation, as Palamon himself tells him: " 'Cosyn, for sothe, of this opinioun / Thow hast a veyn ymaginacioun. / This prison caused me nat for to crye' " (1093-1095). Clinging to a fatalistic acceptance, he considers life as good as over and thinks Palamon errs in reacting humanly to any human situation. In effect, by cutting himself off from even the small part of the outside world open to his view and by rebuking his friend for feeling human emotions, Arcite denies life and the power of the goddess Natura.

Chaucer immediately demonstrates that Arcite follows this apathetic fatalism only because life has not intruded upon his sensibilities. As I have pointed out, in the beginning Palamon achieves a measure of equanimity by making the outside world a part of his existence in prison. Arcite, on the contrary, maintains philosophical equilibrium by denying life and refusing to recognize its claim upon him. For Arcite, this stoical pessimism is not a real solution to his prison situation. Instead, it represents the easy way out of anguish and woe, of forgetting all that resembles life. It is the path of least resistance. The acid test of such an attitude is whether it can endure when it is inescapably confronted with the living world, and Arcite's attitude cannot. When he looks out the window and sees Emily, his resignation begins to crumble. At this point he realizes that he is not yet dead, that the will to live again is strong within him. Ironically, he phrases the realization in the inverted and contradictory terms of the courtly love code as he swears, first, that he is slain by Emily's beauty and, further, that he will die if he cannot see her (1118-1122). When Palamon and Arcite bicker over which of the two is "fals" in loving the other's lady, Arcite almost forgets his former resignation. He argues heatedly and at length over a lover's freedom from authority, adding a hopeless postscript by way of afterthought:

> "And eek it is nat likly al thy lyf
> To stonden in hir grace; namoore shal I;
> For wel thou woost thyselven, verraily,
> That thou and I be dampned to prisoun
> Perpetuelly; us gayneth no raunsoun."   (1172-1176)

Even though Arcite admits that " 'we stryve as dide the houndes for the boon' " (1177), his moral tag does not solve his love problem, for "greet was the strif and long bitwix hem tweye" (1187). Thus life in all the intensity of young and passionate love intrudes upon him, and he cannot reject it.

Arcite resembles Palamon in one vital detail: he, too, falls under the dominion of the conventions of courtly love as he argues jealously and violently with Palamon about love's relation to positive and natural law. Arcite has no preliminary vision of Venus as a powerful, beneficent agent in God's order. Thus, from the beginning his love is ruled by the capricious and "geery" Venus of courtly love tradition. Since love shakes him from his apathy, he equates love with life. This is quite in accord with the tenets of Natura, whose fundamental law is love. But he further equates life with the barren atmosphere of prison, an attitude which is wholly opposed to Natura's principles. Chaucer focuses on Arcite's perverted view of life when Perotheus gains the knight's release from prison. Though Perotheus' entreaty gains Arcite the freedom that is his as a living creature of Nature, Arcite responds to his release by making great dole, insisting that leaving the prison – and Emily – means damnation. At this point, because of the influence of Venus, the courtly and artificial

goddess, Arcite's values are quite reversed. Natura's earth becomes "helle" (1226); Theseus' dungeon, "paradys" (1237).
Arcite blames the goddess Fortuna for casting him down and
favoring Palamon (" 'Wel hath Fortune yturned thee the dys' "
– 1238), and he cries out in self-pity, inveighing against the very
act which offers him the grace of life:

> "But I, that am exiled and bareyne
> Of alle grace, and in so greet dispeir,
> That ther nys erthe, water, fir, ne eir,
> Ne creature that of hem maked is,
> That may me helpe or doon confort in this,
> Wel oughte I sterve in wanhope and distresse.
> Farwel my lif, my lust, and my gladnesse!" (1244-1250)

At this rebellious moment he launches into an extended speech
based on Boethian precepts of acceptance, a speech which
Chaucer uses with fine irony, to indicate that blindly falling into
an attitude (as does Arcite) is not at all the same as thoughtfully
seeking acceptance of a situation (as does Boethius and, ultimately, as do the other characters in the tale). The philosophy
underlying Arcite's speech is flawless Boethianism.[19] Arcite points
out the basic Boethian tenet that the providence of God follows
a plan which operates for the good of man, though this plan is
inscrutable to mortals, who bring disaster upon themselves by
working counter to it. Further, he laments that men in their
inability to fathom the divine plan often long for the delights of
false felicity (1265-1267). Arcite admits that he once wished to
escape from prison (1268-1271), but he now believes that he
should not have wished this because only in prison – near Emily
– can he live in bliss (1272-1274). For at least two reasons
Arcite's Boethian speech does not ring true. First, his invective
against Fortuna's bounty toward Palamon and her coldness toward him – not to mention his flood of self-pity – precludes the
philosophical acceptance to which he gives lip-service. Second,
Arcite applies Boethian principles to a topsy-turvy situation.
Boethian philosophy demands harmony between man and Natura

---

[19] For analysis of Arcite's speech as Boethian philosophy, see Lumiansky,
Of Sondry Folk, pp. 38-39.

and acceptance of Fortuna. Arcite, on the contrary, uses Boethian terminology to justify wishing to remain in prison, thus denying the power of Natura in her living, outside world. In short, Arcite's later actions, especially his fate at the end of the tale, indicate that he uses Boethius' philosophy to justify pursuing false felicity. This speech serves as Chaucer's conclusive indication that Arcite's fatalistic acceptance of his lot is only a veneer which cracks when life intrudes upon him and which has now completely vanished.

Arcite leaves Athens because he has no choice, but contact with the world does not revivify him as a creature of Natura. Instead, he has bitterly acknowledged Fortuna as the fickle governor of the universe and of his personal destiny, and the outside world affects him like poison instead of the elixir of life. Because he cannot forget Emily he is afflicted with the "loveris maladye / Of Hereos" (1373-1374); and, with faint suggestion of a deeper ill, he becomes "rather lyk manye, / Engendred of humour malencolik, / Biforen . . ." (1374-1376). When Mercury summons Arcite back to Athens, he goes transformed into almost a different being by Fortuna and the unstable Venus: "turned was al up so doun / Bothe habit and eek disposicioun / Of hym" (1377-1379), and he "saugh his visage al in another kynde" (1401). Thus he returns to the stronghold of the fickle goddess.

He goes, however, in a manner that leaves him vulnerable to the beneficent power of Natura. In joining Theseus' household, Arcite "cladde hym as a povre laborer" (1409) and "at the gate he profreth his survyse / To drugge and drawe, what so men wol devyse" (1415-1416). He performs humble tasks which bring him close contact with the natural world ("Wel koude he hewen wode, and water bere" – 1422). At this point Arcite is like Griselda at her father's house: making no attempt to work out a philosophy, he sheds the trappings of pomp and courtliness and stays close to the essential stuff of life. When Theseus promotes him to squire, he continues to live discreetly and happily. He is no longer victim to the ills attendant upon courtly love, and he expresses no hint of conventional lamentation over Emily and her unattainability. Chaucer says that he is in "blisse" (1449) and implies that his joy comes from his whole condition of life, not only from his nearness to Emily. For the first time Arcite recognizes the charm of the natural world, and his new affinity with the realm of Natura draws him compellingly to honor the springtime:

> ... firy Phebus riseth up so bright
> That al the orient laugheth of the light,
> And with his stremes dryeth in the greves
> The silver dropes hangynge on the leves.
> And Arcita, that in the court roial
> With Theseus is squier principal,
> Is risen and looketh on the myrie day.
> And for doon his observaunce to May,
> Remembrynge on the poynt of his desir,
> He on a courser, startlynge as the fir,
> Is riden into the feeldes hym to pleye,
> Out of the court, were it a myle or tweye.   (1493-1504)

His selfless delight in Natura's gladsome month causes him to burst into spontaneous song: " 'May, with alle thy floures and thy grene, / Welcome be thou, faire, fresshe May, / In hope that I som grene gete may' " (1510-1512). He seems on his way towards rejuvenation. But Chaucer has shortly before warned that Arcite is under the dominion of Fortuna, and his happiness is doomed from the start (Arcite "litel wiste how ny that was his care, / Til that Fortune had broght him in the snare" – 1489-1490). Thus "geery Venus", changeable even as Fortuna is changeable, fills him with discontent, and he behaves once more like the courtly lover, "Now in the crope, now doun in the breres, / Now up, now doun, as boket in a welle" (1533-1534). Inveighing against his state of servitude, he attributes his condition to the irrational cruelty of the gods (1543, 1559). He phrases his lover's plaint in conventional courtly style and blames the worst of his caitiff state upon love. Fortuna's pattern takes effect once more as Palamon crawls from the bushes, incensed, and confronts Arcite. From this point on, Arcite is irrevocably under the dominion of Fortuna.

Theseus announces that Fortuna will decide the winner of the tourney and of Emily, and Arcite's energies are directed henceforth towards winning Fortuna's palm in battle. By swearing allegiance to Mars, Arcite renounces any lingering affinity with the goddess Natura. The temple to Mars which Theseus commissions represents a malignant perversion of Natura's glory. The setting which the fresco portrays is natural, but it is a landscape devoid of life:

> First on the wal was peynted a forest,
> In which ther dwelleth neither man ne best,
> With knotty, knarry, bareyne trees olde,
> Of stubbes sharpe and hidouse to biholde,
> In which ther ran a rumbel in a swough,
> As though a storm sholde bresten every bough.   (1975-1980)

The temple is not made of natural elements but of "burned steel", with a door of adamant and pillars of iron. It is filled with terrible forms of bloody and unnatural death: "The smylere with the knyf under the cloke" (1999); "The tresoun of the mordrynge in the bedde; / The open werre, with woundes al bibledde" (2001-2002); "The sleere of hymself yet saugh I ther" (2005); "The nayl ydryven in the shode anyght; / The colde deeth, with mouth gapyng upright" (2007-2008); "The careyne in the busk, with throte ycorve" (2013); "The hunte strangled with the wilde beres; / The sowe freten the child right in the cradel; / The cook yscalded, for al his longe ladel" (2018-2020). The statue of Mars is magnificent but terrible – grimly armed, with celestial figures of divination above his head and a man-eating wolf at his feet. In paying homage to this grisly god, Arcite entreats him as the agent of Fortuna, who " 'hem fortunest as thee lyst devyse' " (2377). Further, Arcite appeals to Mars as a fellow sufferer in love, as the illicit lover of Venus whom Vulcan caught with the goddess and humiliated before the Olympian deities. Since Mars knows the anguish of courtly love, he should help Arcite, who is also afflicted with its woes: " 'Thanne help me, lord, tomorwe in my bataille, / For thilke fyr that whilom brente thee, / As wel as thilke fyr now brenneth me' " (2402-2404). Arcite's reference to this episode in Mars' history puts Mars on a level with Antigamus, whom Alain denounces as throwing askew the divine plan for love in the universe of created beings.[20] In summary,

[20]   *De Planctu*: PL, CCX. 302.80-303.43.

the description of the temple, with its emphasis on sudden death, foreshadows Arcite's end as one of those violently slain in the service of Mars; and Arcite's orison foreshadows that he is not to win Emily, who is a votaress of Natura.

Arcite's victory in battle is the gift of Fortuna. When Arcite overcomes Palamon by force of numbers, Theseus declares, " 'Arcite of Thebes shal have Emelie, / That by his fortune hath hire faire ywonne' " (2658-2659). Even Emily follows the "favour of Fortune" (2682) and regards Arcite with acquisitive interest. Arcite is at the top of Fortuna's wheel. His plummeting descent is as sudden as his rise, for the "furie infernal . . . / From Pluto sent at requeste of Saturne" (2684-2685) appears instantly to knock him from his horse. When the fury, agent of death and thus of Fortuna, mangles Arcite so that he can no longer function physically, Natura's last tenuous hold upon him is broken: "Nature hath now no dominacioun. / And certeinly, ther Nature wol nat wirche, / Fare wel phisik! go ber the man to chirche!" (2758-2760). Though Arcite, at the instant of his downfall, has failed to transcend Fortuna and thus rise to inner peace, his dying speech suggests that the knight's end is ambiguous. Arcite begins hopelessly, with lamentation over his unfulfilled passion for Emily; and he proceeds to bitter questioning of life's universals. Since the basic idea of Fortuna precludes any concept of order or reason, Arcite approaches death bewildered by the life through which he has passed: " 'What is this world? what asketh men to have? / Now with his love, now in his colde grave / Allone, withouten any compaignye' " (2777-2779). Yet, strangely, with his last breath he apprehends a vision of glorious and perfect human love as he humbly apologizes for his "strif and rancour" and his "jalousye" (2784, 2785) and recognizes in Palamon the highest qualities befitting a lover – " 'That is to seyen, trouthe, honour, knyghthede, / Wysdom, humblesse, estaat, and heigh kynrede, / Fredom, and al that longeth to that art' " (2789-2791). Perhaps Chaucer suggests that he dies with something of a realization that the loving power of Natura is more efficacious for human happiness than the capricious rule of Fortuna, even though he sees no beneficent order in the created world such as the other characters see at the end of the tale. At any rate, the bitterness of his outcry, "'What is this world? what asketh men to have?'" (2777), is somewhat allayed by his dying entreaty that Emily "'Foryet nat Palamon, the gentil man'" (2797).

The heavenly quarrel scene provoked by the orisons of Emily and the two lovers deserves brief consideration. The most important member of the hierarchy is Saturn, who does not appear in the *Teseida*. Chaucer introduces him as the Olympian *deus ex machina*, who enters to resolve the conflict on the divine level just as Egeus does on the human level. Saturn, an exponent of disorder, strife, and disunity, is the opposite of Egeus, and the god's pleased recital of his own responsibilities reads like a roll call of the horrors in the temple of Mars:

> "Myn is the drenchyng in the see so wan;
> Myn is the prison in the derke cote;
> Myn is the stranglyng and hangyng by the throte,
> The murmure and the cherles rebellyng,
> The groynynge, and the pryvee empoysonyng . . . ."   (2456-2460)

We should expect Saturn to foster conflict, not to resolve it. But Chaucer states that in this instance Saturn acts "agayn his kynde" (2451). That is, he acts against his own nature – rancorous and belligerent – in order to act in accordance with Natura, the principle of order in the natural world, and bring concord to his children. Further, he arbitrates in order that he may appease the heavenly representatives of both Natura and Fortuna. His promise to Venus that Palamon "'Shal have his lady'" (2472) foreshadows the end of "parfit joye" (3072) for Palamon and Emily when they marry. His promise that "'Mars shal helpe his knyght'" (2473) foreshadows Arcite's tournament victory at the hand of Fortuna. Since there is such affinity for blood between Saturn and Mars and since Saturn is such a lover of human distress, perhaps it also foreshadows Arcite's sudden fatal tumble from Fortuna's wheel. In short, Saturn, the archetypal god, acts "agayn his kynde" – in accord with Natura's love of concord – to resolve the divine strife, thus making possible resolution of the conflict on the human level.

The philosophical theme of the tale and the resolution of the Natura-Fortuna contest depend ultimately upon a single speech – Theseus' bond-of-love oration. Before the occasion for this speech, the principles of Fortuna seem victorious over the precepts of Natura. Arcite is dead because Fortuna has toppled him from her wheel; Theseus has pillaged Natura's grove to honor Arcite's death at the hand of Fortuna; and the love situation of Palamon and Emily, both overcome by grief, has reached an impasse. After uneventful years all the complications suddenly resolve themselves when Theseus delivers a lengthy lecture. Palamon and Emily become reconciled to Arcite's death; they marry happily; the kingdoms of Athens and Thebes unite. The ending to the tale is not hastily drummed up, for Chaucer begins to prepare for Theseus' final speech when he brings Egeus into the tale. Theseus' father plays a much more prominent role in the *Teseida* than he does in Chaucer's narrative. In Boccaccio's poem Egeo is king of Athens. He appears frequently and talks much, with his every appearance attended by pomp and ceremony. Egeo is as stunned as everyone else by Arcite's death, and the words he speaks pass unnoticed amid the bitter lamenting (XII. 9-11). Chaucer's Egeus appears for the first time after Arcite's death, heralded only as Theseus' "olde fader" (2838). Unlike Boccaccio's Egeo, Egeus plays a vital functional role: just as Saturn arises to resolve the heavenly conflict, so Egeus enters to pave the way for resolution of the human difficulties.[21] The consolation which Egeus offers to Theseus demands, at best, unflinching acceptance of the world as a "thurfare ful of wo" (2847); yet Egeus' counsel contains the germinal idea from which Theseus evolves his ultimate philosophy, the Boethian doctrine of Natura's beneficent flux and change:

> "Right as ther dyed nevere man," quod he,
> "That he ne lyvede in erthe in some degree,
> Right so ther lyvede never man," he seyde,
> "In al this world, that som tyme he ne deyde."   (2843-2846)

[21] Frost, p. 299, gives Egeus' speech central importance for its "direct, simple, and uncompromising expression" of the tragic view which Frost sees in the tale.

Theseus recognizes the truth in Egeus' words and is consoled ("No man myghte gladen Theseus, / Savynge his olde fader Egeus" – 2837-2838), but he does not immediately support Egeus' remarks with a polished Boethian exposition. That he cannot do so, in fact, constitutes one of Chaucer's primary philosophical points. Theseus cannot instantly assimilate his father's counsel; instead, he meets the immediate demand of the moment by preparing the funeral.

Only later – much later, Chaucer indicates – when grief is no longer fresh and when Theseus himself is older, can the duke evolve his own ordered view of the universe from his father's advice. He brings the ideas in Egeus' brief counsel to explicit statement as he points out, with examples from the world of Natura and of man ("the ook" – 3017; "the harde stoon" – 3021; "the brode ryver" – 3024; "the grete tounes" – 3025), the impossibility of earthly immortality:

> Of man and womman seen we wel also
> That nedes, in oon of these termes two,
> This is to seyn, in youthe or elles age,
> He moot be deed, the kyng as shal a page;
> Som in his bed, som in the depe see,
> Som in the large feeld, as men may see;
> Ther helpeth noght, al goth that ilke weye.   (3027-3033)

He expands Egeus' dictum that " 'Deeth is an ende of every worldly soore' " (2849) as he points out that " 'certeinly a man hath moost honour / To dyen in his excellence and flour, / Whan he is siker of his goode name' " (3047-3049) and that " 'gladder oghte his freend been of his deeth, / Whan with honour up yolden is his breeth, / Than whan his name apalled is for age' " (3051-3053). But Theseus transcends Egeus' philosophy because he adds a new dimension – love. For Theseus the key is not – as it is for Egeus – grim acceptance of "this worldes transmutacioun" (2839). Rather, Theseus bases his philosophy on the creative love of God, the "Firste Moevere" who, through his "vicaire" Natura, endows the world with eternal order and direction. Since " 'greet was th' effect, and heigh was his entente' " (2989) when the First Mover " 'first made the faire cheyne of love' " (2988) which binds objects and creatures of the natural world to each other and to God, Theseus realizes that man must achieve not only acceptance but good from every human experience. Only at this moment does Chaucer reveal Theseus as capable of speaking with such depth of eloquent understanding. Only after the "lengthe of certeyn yeres" (2967) can Theseus build a stable philosophy from the austere counsel of his father. Theseus' speech represents the sum of his years and experience, and I think Chaucer's point is that Theseus could not have made such a powerful affirmative declaration before this instant in the tale.

Indeed, every characterization in the tale contributes to Chaucer's implicit assertion that ability to cope with God's ordered universe comes with age and understanding. "As sooth is seyd, elde hath greet avantage; / In elde is bothe wysdom and usage; / Men may the olde atrenne, and noght atrede" (2447-2449): these platitudes may seem rather ironic since Saturn, in whose scene they appear, is anything but the benevolent grandfatherly type. Nonetheless, these lines have their impact in the tale. For instance, they help to explain the peculiar similiarity between Saturn and Egeus. It seems to me that Chaucer, introducing Saturn independently of his source and de-emphasizing and sharply focusing the role of Egeus, creates a definite parallel between the two characters. Both Saturn and Egeus are figures of patriarchal majesty, and both appear almost from nowhere at a moment of crisis when the established ruler cannot cope with a certain situation. When mighty Jupiter is at his wits' end, Saturn – older than the father of the gods – arbitrates the quarrel with powerful authority; when Theseus and his kingdom are overcome with grief, old Egeus – wiser than the potentate of Athens – offers counsel and comfort. Saturn knows "so manye of aventures olde" (2444) that he "foond in his olde experience" (2445) a satisfactory resolution to the heavenly strife. Egeus can show Theseus consoling "ensamples and liknesse" (2842) because he "knew this worldes transmutacioun, / As he hadde seyn it chaunge both up and doun, / Joye after wo, and wo after gladnesse" (2839-2841). Thus, these two figures provide a background for Chaucer's concern with age and experience in the tale as a whole, for he introduces them as symbols grimly suggestive of archetypal authority and wisdom.[22]

Theseus looks to his own age and experience ("'Ther nedeth noght noon auctoritee t'allegge, / For it is preeved by experience, / But that me list declaren my sentence'" – 3000-3002) as sufficient authority for asserting his philosophical views: "'Thanne is it wysdom, as it thynketh me, / To maken vertu of necessitee, / And take it weel that we may nat eschue'" (3041-3043). Palamon and Emily also gain wisdom and understanding. They, too, endure "the lengthe of certeyn yeres" until their grief over the outrages of Fortuna lessens and they can accept the benevolent order of the natural universe as Theseus explains it. They prove their acceptance in their marriage, which fulfills their function as creatures of Natura and which creates from sorrow "'O parfit joye, lastynge everemo'" (3072). Arcite alone of the characters speaks without experience, and he alone perishes by the hand of Fortuna, baffled by the universe. Though I do not hint that Chaucer moralizes, I do assert that the charactizations, the deliberately lengthy periods of time, and the outcome of the tale all give dramatic focus to a concept inherent in Boethian thought – that experience and understanding are prerequisites to philosophical acceptance.

To sum up, Chaucer in the "Knight's Tale" sets Natura and Fortuna in an opposition which reinforces the tale's Boethian philosophy of the First Mover, Providence, and Destiny. Second, as in the *Book of the Duchess*, though with greater complexity in the working out of his scheme, Chaucer equates Natura with Life and Fortuna with Death. Third, Chaucer sets the Venus of courtly love tradition in opposition to the Goddess of Kind, judging courtly tradition incompatible with the fundamental tenets of Natura. Fourth, Chaucer shapes the conflict between the deities to establish the philosophical point that a life in accord

---

[22]   Critics generally consider Saturn and Theseus – not Saturn and Egeus – as analogous characters. See, for example, Muscatine, who discusses Saturn and Theseus as representing disorder and order respectively (p. 929). See also Baum, who discusses Saturn and Theseus as presiding over the heavenly and earthly rivalry (p. 96).

with Natura and an acceptance of the Boethian universe do not result from mere physical existence but from thought, age, and understanding. These statements do not attempt to reduce the tale to a four-point outline. Rather they indicate that the delicate relationship between Natura and Fortuna as it is focused in the characters affects Chaucer's plot, structure, characterization, philosophical exposition, and use of medieval courtly conventions.

With Natura and Fortuna reinforcing the Boethian philosophy and serving as norms for human action in the "Knight's Tale", just as they do for the pagans in the *Troilus*, we see that Chaucer's view of the goddesses is ambiguous, and the use he makes of them depends upon his subject. In narratives with strong Christian backgrounds, such as the "Physician's Tale" and the "Clerk's Tale" – stories dealing with Christian virtue and patience respectively – both deities are sharply limited, and the characters' human task is that of asserting the strength of godlike love to overcome forces both of limited malevolence (Fortuna) and limited beneficence (Natura). Though up to a point the tales could be read as allegorical conflicts between Fortuna-characters and Natura-characters, the triumph of love over both deities reinforces the human level. On the other hand, in poems in which the dominant note is Boethian, as in the "Knight's Tale" and the *Book of the Duchess*, Fortuna and Natura assume a degree of absoluteness and function as the alternatives for human resolution. The *Troilus* includes suggestions of both absoluteness and limitation, as does the *Parliament of Fowls*. Within each tale examined at length, the view of Natura and Fortuna is consistent, with variations from tale to tale. Though the dramatic opposition of the goddesses is admittedly not vital to an interpretation of the entire Chaucer canon, it appears frequently and forcefully enough to reveal new depths in a number of the narratives.

BIBLIOGRAPHY

TEXTS:

Alanus de Insulis, *Anticlaudianus*, ed. R. Bossuat (Paris, 1955).

——, *The Anticlaudian of Alain de Lille*, transl. William Hafner Cornog (Philadelphia, 1935).

——, *The Complaint of Nature*, transl. Douglas M. Moffatt (New York, 1908).

——, *Opera Omnia* in *Patrologia Latina*, Vol. CCX, ed. J. P. Migne (Montrouge, 1855).

Boccaccio, Giovanni, *Teseida della Nozze d'Emilia*, ed. Aurelio Roncaglia (= *Scrittori d'Italia*, Vol. CLXXXV) (Bari, 1941).

Chaucer, Geoffrey, *The Works of Geoffrey Chaucer*, ed. F. N. Robinson, 2nd ed. (Cambridge, Mass., 1957).

Gower, John, *The Works of John Gower*, 4 vols., ed. G. C. Macaulay (Oxford, 1901).

Guillaume de Lorris and Jean de Meun, *Le Roman de la Rose*, 5 vols., ed. Ernest Langlois. *Société des Anciens Textes Français* (Paris, 1914-1924).

Guillaume de Machaut, *Musikalische Werke*, ed. Friedrich Ludwig (Wiesbaden, 1954).

——, *Oeuvres*, 3 vols., ed. Ernest Hoepffner. *Société des Anciens Textes Français* (Paris, 1908-1921).

Livius, Titus, *Ab Urbe Condita*. Loeb Classical Library (New York, 1922).

CRITICISMS:

apRoberts, Robert, "The Central Episode in Chaucer's *Troilus*", *PMLA*, LXXVII (1962), 373-385.

Baker, Donald C., "The Poet of Love and the *Parlement of Foules*", *University of Mississippi Studies in English*, II (1961), 78-110.

Baum, Paull F., *Chaucer: A Critical Appreciation* (Durham, N.C., 1958).

Bennett, J. A. W., *The Parlement of Foules: An Interpretation* (Oxford, 1957).

Bethurum, Dorothy, "Chaucer's Point of View as Narrator in the Love Poems", *PMLA*, LXXIV (1959), 511-520.

Bloomfield, Morton W., "Distance and Predestination in *Troilus and Criseyde*", *PMLA*, LXXII (1957), 14-26.

Bronson, Bertrand H., "The *Parlement of Foules* Revisited", *ELH*, XV (1948), 247-260.

——, *In Search of Chaucer* (Toronto, 1960).

Bryan, W. F. and Germaine Dempster (eds.), *Sources and Analogues of Chaucer's "Canterbury Tales"* (New York, 1958).

Cate, W. A., "The Problem of the Origin of the Griselda Story", *SP*, XXIX (1932), 389-405.

Chute, Marchette, *Geoffrey Chaucer of England* (New York, 1946).

Clark, John W., "Dante and the Epilogue of the *Troilus*", *JEGP*, L (1951), 1-10.

Coulton, G. F., *Chaucer and His England*, 4th ed. (London, 1927).

Curry, Walter Clyde, *Chaucer and the Medieval Sciences* (New York, 1926).

——, "Arcite's Intellect", *JEGP*, XXIX (1930), 83-99.

——, "Destiny in Chaucer's *Troilus*", *PMLA*, XLV (1930), 129-168.

David, Alfred, "The Hero of the *Troilus*", *Speculum*, XXXVII (1962), 566-581.

DeLage, G. Raynaud, *Alain de Lille* (Montreal, 1951).

Dempster, Germaine, *Dramatic Irony in Chaucer* (Stanford, 1932).

Dodd, William G., *Courtly Love in Chaucer and Gower* (Gloucester, Mass., 1913).

Donaldson, E. T. (ed.), *Chaucer's Poetry: An Anthology for the Modern Reader* (New York, 1958).

Dunning, T. P., "God and Man in *Troilus and Criseyde*", *English and Medieval Studies*, ed. Norman Davis and C. L. Wrenn (London, 1962), pp. 164-182.

Fabin, Madeleine, "On Chaucer's *Anelida and Arcite*", *MLN*, XXXIV (1919), 266-272.

Fairchild, Hoxie N., "Active Arcite, Contemplative Palamon", *JEGP*, XXVI (1927), 285-293.

Frank, Robert W., Jr., "Structure and Meaning in the *Parlement of Foules*", *PMLA*, LXXI (1956), 530-539.

French, R. D., *A Chaucer Handbook*, 2nd ed. (New York, 1947).

French, W. H., "The Lovers in the 'Knight's Tale' ", *JEGP*, XLVIII (1949), 320-328.

Frost, William, "An Interpretation of Chaucer's 'Knight's Tale' ", *RES*, XXV (1949), 289-304.

Gaylord, Alan, "Uncle Pandarus as Lady Philosophy", *Papers of the Michigan Academy of Science, Arts, and Letters*, XLVI (1960), 571-595.

Giffin, Mary, *Studies on Chaucer and His Audience* (Hull, Quebec, 1956).

Green, Marian N., "Christian Implications of Knighthood and Courtly Love in Chaucer's *Troilus*", *Delaware Notes*, XXX (1957), 57-92.

Green, Richard Hamilton, "Alain of Lille's *De Planctu Naturae*", *Speculum*, XXXI (1956), 649-674.

Griffith, Dudley David, *The Origin of the Griselda Story* (Seattle, 1931).

Gunn, Alan F., *The Mirror of Love: A Reinterpretation of "The Romance of the Rose"* (Lubbock, 1952).

Ham, Eugene B., "Knight's Tale 38", *ELH*, XVII (1950), 252-261.

Heninger, S. K., Jr., "The Concept of Order in Chaucer's 'Clerk's Tale' ", *JEGP*, LVI (1957), 382-395.

Hulbert, J. R., "What Was Chaucer's Aim in the 'Knight's Tale' "?, *SP*, XXVI (1929), 375-385.

Huppé, Bernard and D. W. Robertson, *Fruyt and Chaf: Studies in Chaucer's Allegories* (Princeton, 1963).

Jefferson, Bernard L., *Chaucer and the Consolation of Philosophy of Boethius* (Princeton, 1917).

Jordan, Robert M., "The Narrator in Chaucer's *Troilus*", *ELH*, XXV (1958), 237-257.

Kirby, Thomas A., *Chaucer's Troilus: A Study in Courtly Love* (Baton Rouge, 1940).

Kittredge, G. L., *Chaucer and His Poetry* (Cambridge, 1956).

Knowlton, E. C., "The Goddess Nature in Early Periods", *JEGP*, XIX (1920), 224-253.

——, "Nature in Middle English", *JEGP*, XX (1921), 186-207.

——, "Nature in Old French", *MP*, XX (1922), 309-329.

——, "Nature in Early German", *JEGP*, XXIV (1925), 409-412.

Lewis, C. S., "What Chaucer really did to *Il Filostrato*", *Essays and Studies*, XVII (1932), 56-75.

——, *The Allegory of Love: A Study in Medieval Tradition* (Oxford, 1936; reprint, 1948).

Lounsbury, Thomas R., *Studies in Chaucer*, 3 vols. (New York, 1892).

Lovejoy, A. O., *The Great Chain of Being* (Cambridge, Mass., 1936).

Lumiansky, R. M., "Chaucer's *Parlement of Foules*: A Philosophical Interpretation", *RES*, XXIV (1948), 81-89.

——, "The Function of the Proverbial Monitory Elements in Chaucer's *Troilus and Criseyde*", *Tulane Studies in English*, II (1950), 5-48.

——, *Of Sondry Folk: The Dramatic Principle in the Canterbury Tales* (Austin, 1955).

——, "The Bereaved Narrator in Chaucer's *The Book of the Duchess*", *Tulane Studies in English*, IX (1959), 5-17.

Magoun, F. P., Jr., "*Canterbury Tales* A 11", *MLN*, LXX (1955), 399.

Malone, Kemp, *Chapters on Chaucer* (Baltimore, 1951).

Marckwardt, A. H., *Characterization in Chaucer's "Knight's Tale"* (Ann Arbor, 1947).

Mayo, Robert D., "The Trojan Background of the *Troilus*", *ELH*, IX (1942), 245-256.

McDonald, Charles O., "An Interpretation of Chaucer's *Parlement of Foules*", *Speculum*, XXX (1955), 444-457.

Meech, Sanford B., *Design in Chaucer's Troilus* (Syracuse, 1959).

Muscatine, Charles, "Form, Texture, and Meaning in Chaucer's 'Knight's Tale' ", *PMLA*, LXV (1950), 911-929.

——, *Chaucer and the French Tradition* (Berkeley, 1957).

Owen, Charles A., Jr., "The Role of the Narrator in the *Parlement of Foules*", *CE*, XIV (1953), 264-269.

Patch, Howard R., "Troilus on Predestination", *JEGP*, XVII (1918), 399-422.

——, "Chaucer and Lady Fortune", *MLR*, XXII (1927), 377-388.

——, *The Goddess Fortuna in Medieval Literature* (Cambridge, Mass., 1927).

——, "Troilus on Determinism", *Speculum*, VI (1931), 225-243.

——, *The Tradition of Boethius* (New York, 1935).

——, *On Rereading Chaucer* (Cambridge, Mass., 1939).

Pratt, Robert A., "Chaucer's Use of the *Teseida*", *PMLA*, LXII (1947), 598-621.

——, " 'Joye after Wo' in the *Knight's Tale*", *JEGP*, LVII (1958), 416-423.

Robertson, D. W., "Chaucerian Tragedy", *ELH*, XIX (1952), 1-37.

Root, R. K., *The Poetry of Chaucer* (New York, 1906).

Ruggiers, Paul G., "Some Philosophical Aspects of the *Knight's Tale*", *CE*, XIX (1958), 296-302.

Scaglione, Aldo A., *Love and Nature in the Late Middle Ages* (Berkeley, 1963).

Severs, J. Burke, "The Literary Relationships of Chaucer's *Clerkes Tale*", *Yale Studies in English*, XCVI (New York, 1942).

Shanley, James, L., "The *Troilus* and Christian Love", *ELH*, VI (1939), 271-281.

Silverstein, Theodore, "Chaucer's Modest and Homely Poem: *The Parlement*", *MP*, XVI (1959), 270-276.

Slaughter, Eugene Edward, *Virtue According to Love – in Chaucer* (New York, 1957).

Sledd, James, "The *Clerk's Tale*: The Monsters and the Critics", *MP*, LI (1953), 73-82.

Socola, Edward M., "Chaucer's Development of Fortune in the 'Monk's Tale' ", *JEGP*, XLIX (1950), 159-171.

Speirs, John, *Chaucer the Maker* (London, 1951).

Stillwell, Gardiner, "Unity and Comedy in Chaucer's *Parlement of Foules*", *JEGP*, XLIX (1950), 470-495.

——, "Chaucer's Eagles and Their Choice on February 14", *JEGP*, LIII (1954), 546-561.

Stroud, Theodore A., "Boethius' Influence on Chaucer's *Troilus*", *MP*, XLIX (1951), 1-9.

Tatlock, J. S. P., *The Development and Chronology of Chaucer's Works* (London, 1907).

—— and Arthur G. Kennedy, *A Concordance to the Complete Works of Geoffrey Chaucer and to the Romaunt of the Rose* (Washington, 1927).

ten Brink, Bernhard, *History of English Literature*, 3 vols. (London, 1901-1914).

Tupper, Frederick, "Chaucer's Bed's Head", *MLN*, XXX (1915), 5-12.

Webb, Henry J., "A Reinterpretation of Chaucer's Theseus", *RES*, XXIII (1947), 289-296.

Wilson, H. S., "The 'Knight's Tale' and the *Teseida* Again", *UTQ*, XVIII (1949), 131-146.

Wright, Herbert G., *Boccaccio in England from Chaucer to Tennyson* (London, 1957).

Young, Karl, "The Maidenly Virtues of Chaucer's Virginia", *Speculum* XVI (1941), 340-349.

DATE DUE

GAYLORD

PRINTED IN U.S.A.